FERNAND DUMONT

Fernand Dumont

A Sociologist Turns to Theology

GREGORY BAUM

McGill-Queen's University Press
Montreal & Kingston • London • Ithaca

© McGill-Queen's University Press 2015

ISBN 978-0-7735-4542-7 (cloth)
ISBN 978-0-7735-8245-3 (ePDF)
ISBN 978-0-7735-8255-2 (ePUB)

Legal deposit second quarter 2015
Bibliothèque nationale du Québec

Printed in Canada on acid-free paper that is 100% ancient forest
free (100% post-consumer recycled), processed chlorine free

McGill-Queen's University Press acknowledges the support of the
Canada Council for the Arts for our publishing program. We also
acknowledge the financial support of the Government of Canada
through the Canada Book Fund for our publishing activities.

Library and Archives Canada Cataloguing in Publication

Baum, Gregory, 1923–
[Fernand Dumont. English]
Fernand Dumont: a sociologist turns to theology / Gregory Baum.

Translation of: Fernand Dumont.
Includes bibliographical references and index.
Issued in print and electronic formats.
ISBN 978-0-7735-4542-7 (bound). – ISBN 978-0-7735-8245-3 (ePDF). –
ISBN 978-0-7735-8255-2 (ePUB)

1. Dumont, Fernand, 1927–1997. Institution de la théologie.
2. Christianity – Philosophy. 3. Theologians. 4. Faith.
5. Sociologists – Québec (Province) – Biography. I. Title.
II. Title: Fernand Dumont. English

BT40.B3813 2015   230.01   C2015-900770-4
                                         C2015-900771-2

This book was typeset by Interscript in 10.5/13.5 Sabon.

Contents

Preface

Gregory Baum is surely one of the most honest, sympathetic, and humble theological thinkers the Catholic Church has been granted over the fifty years since the Second Vatican Council offered its profound challenge to the Church to be "the Church in the World."

Always committed to thinking with the Church, in the Church, and for the Church, Baum has equally been committed to exploring the universal and the particular call for human beings to become fully human – individually, socially and institutionally. He became one of the Church's most direct and inclusive explorers of the Gospel imperative to "go out to the whole world." Baum accepted the imperative as a summons to learn from the world, bring it the spirit of openness and resist its dark side so damaging to human life. With the Second Vatican Council he respected the engagement in the hearts of all genuine seekers.

In this spirit Baum met and came to know the work of Fernand Dumont, a sociologist and philosopher recognized in Quebec as a brilliant public intellectual. Baum acknowledges in his introductory chapter that this meeting was not a case of love at first sight – even though his first sight of Dumont was in connection with the work examined in these pages. Baum acknowledges he had to grow into his appreciation of

Dumont. He tells us how he met Dumont and this work in the doctoral examination of Dumont, who, as a sociologist of accomplishment, had chosen late in his life to seek a doctorate in theology from Laval University. Here is how Baum describes the context:

> I was invited to become one of the examiners of his dissertation, yet because his approach to theology was so different from the theology with which I was acquainted, I failed to discover the originality of Dumont's work. When I read *Une foi partagée* [a later Dumont book] in 2011, I instantly realized that the author was a great theologian, an original thinker, a courageous Christian philosopher ready to face the challenges of modernity posed to the Christian Faith. I was now eager to reread his doctoral dissertation, published in 1987 as the book *L'institution de la théologie.*

Baum draws a certain parallel between Dumont's magnum opus and John Henry Newman's *An Essay on the Development of Christian Doctrine* (1845). Newman's idea of "doctrinal evolution" – so counter to the defensive and fixated spirit of neo-scholastic theology at the time – provided for "a creative process that allowed the Church to develop its teaching while remaining faithful to its original truth." Baum continues: "Dumont's book introduces ideas that reveal the relevance and fecundity of the Gospel in the context created by modern, secular, pluralistic society." Yet, he concludes, "Dumont's book has not yet been received in the Church."

In the present volume Baum reveals Fernand Dumont as a theologian who is historically located. In creating his theology, Dumont never leaves behind his experience as a child of poor working-class parents nor the methodology used in his sociological studies. Consequently his reading of theological meaning is embedded in the dynamics of human engagement – across cultures as well as in the specific realities of a dynamic Quebec society and its institutions. Quebec prior to the Quiet Revolution; Quebec during the high-water effort to create a distinctive socialist identity for itself as a truly cooperative society in which everyone counted; and contemporary Quebec shaped by a gradual submission to the dominant neoliberal model of social existence and development. These historical phases, Baum suggests, form not only the backdrop but the very ground or matrix of Dumont's theological reflection. He explores what it means to be a Church faithful to its calling that is genuinely engaged with secular culture, sensitive to its best voices and strivings, and at the same time aware of its destructive potential.

Dumont's phenomenology of human life, Baum argues, is in keeping with Maurice Blondel's understanding of the human drama: people moved by an inner dynamic to seek the good and the true to the very limit, witnessing the pull of a nameless Transcendent in their lives. Man is always more than man, Pascal wrote; Dumont added to this, a society is always more than a society. Society, he holds, is also subject to the pull of the Transcendent.

In his dialogue with contemporary culture Dumont has great respect for persons of conscience, be they atheists, agnostics, or believers, because their commitment, their fidelity to conscience, testifies to the summons of the Transcendent in their lives. Here dialogue leads to mutual understanding and the discovery of common values, making possible cooperation in the service of the common good. Dumont feels at home in the pluralistic society. He is not troubled by people with divergent convictions. What troubles him are people who are unreflective, purely utilitarian and uncommitted. With Blondel, Dumont holds that the nameless Transcendent in people's lives is the God revealed in the Scriptures.

It seems to me that the journey to such dialogue has its conditions: the sharing of the foundational value of each person, believer or unbeliever, each a subject, a centre of knowledge, acknowledging full equality, seeking ever wider solidarity, and practicing mutuality in discourse and action. I think this requires faith in, commitment to, and need for an affirmation of the freedom of each one to act on her/his best understanding and choices – and not on the prior decision of any group – including the Church. Each person, religious or not, must be accepted as a subject acting by conscience and not by command.

Freedom, equality, solidarity, and full mutuality as pillars of social aspirations are, in fact, modern and contemporary values shaped as much (or more) by secular discovery and practice as by religious inspiration. Even as Dumont critiques individualism, relativism and false absolutes in society, he is led to recognize that the movement promoting the above-mentioned shared convictions in unrelievable social pluralism can ground, for Catholic believers, an enriched, humbled, and faithful interpretation of the constitutive features of their communal and institutional living: faith, truth, revelation, magisterium, and tradition. Dumont's refreshing treatments of these features of the institutional life of the Catholic Church are addressed and unfolded by Baum crisply and with attractive coherence.

Take truth, for example. Truth is seen by Dumont as not merely an intellectual concept or affirmation but as personal understanding grounded in community and in faith. It forms and refines itself in imagining and feeling, in guiding myths, poetry and vision, in figures, models, and metaphors prior to taking expression in concepts. Truth, in Baum's reading of Dumont, is essentially the relevance of concepts and proclamations to actual living.

Affirming the importance of the cultural context in coming to grasp (or be grasped by) the truth could be seen as a superficial acceptance of cultural factors over timeless truths or simply an adaptation of current fashions. This is not what Dumont has in mind when he claims that truth must be relevant to contemporary culture. In his encyclical "The Joy of the Gospel" Pope Francis makes the same claim:

truth needs to be embedded in a living culture to be effective in believing.

> There are times when the faithful, listening to completely orthodox language, take away something alien to the authentic Gospel of Jesus Christ because that language is alien to their own ways of speaking to and understanding one another. With the holy intent of communicating the truth about God and humanity, we sometimes given them a false god or a human ideal which is not really Christian. In this way, we hold fast to a formulation while failing to convey its substance. (#41)

According to Dumont, as explained by Baum, the Gospel can find expression in terms drawn from different cultures, because biblical truth is more than a series of concepts. Dumont sees the truth of Jesus not only, and not primarily, in what he said, but more especially in what he did. Through his actions, his responses to persons he met, his reactions to challenges and his readiness to suffer, the presence of Jesus evokes in us a conversion of heart and a new grasp of the meaning of life. Inspired by what he said and did, believers find themselves called to freedom from constriction, to transformation from fear to trust, and from primary self-concern to love of others and self-gift.

Because Dumont has reconceived truth in this manner, he is able to offer original interpretations of the mission of theologians, the function of the magisterium, the meaning of Tradition, the place of doctrine in proclamation, and true membership in the Church. Baum shows that in proposing these innovative interpretations Dumont draws upon the faith experiences of the believing community, upon the reading of Scripture by the Fathers and the early Councils, and upon Christian witnesses throughout the ages.

Baum shows that in the sixties and early seventies Dumont supported the Quiet Revolution as a left-leaning social scientist full of hope, while in the eighties, disturbed by the bureaucratization of society, he feared that Quebec was losing its creative spirit and the rootedness in its own culture. Taking into account his entire work, some readers see Dumont as a progressive thinker with utopian aspirations, while others see him as a conservative thinker attached to the communitarian character of traditional society. Baum offers a progressive reading of Dumont, emphasizing the bold vision he had of the future Church.

In offering English-speaking readers access to Dumont's magnum opus, Baum introduces them to hopeful thinking following a learned theological methodology that is biblically based, attentive to tradition and seeks expression in terms of contemporary culture. Baum's presentation encourages us to follow Dumont in fearlessly doing theology in critical dialogue with culture, willing to learn from its insights and values and ready to detect and denounce its dark side: its idolatry, lies and oppressions. The Gospel challenges the given culture, utters the truth about it, and offers healing. Dumont extends an invitation to those in the Church and those who in conscience remain apart from the Church to come together in open, respectful dialogue and joint action in the service of humanity. In offering this author as a model for doing theology at this time, Gregory Baum has done us a great service.

Jack Costello, SJ
Regis College, Toronto

FERNAND DUMONT

I

Introducing Fernand Dumont

I discovered the thought of Fernand Dumont late in life. In June 2011 I decided to ask the department of theological studies of Montreal's Concordia University to allow me to teach a graduate course on Catholic theology in French Quebec. While I had been a professor in the religious studies faculty at McGill University, an anglophone institution, I was an active participant in the francophone Church. I joined la Société canadienne de théologie and was a member of the editorial committee of the francophone revue *Relations*, sponsored by the Jesuit Community. Because of my integration into francophone society, I was unhappy that the theological literature produced by French Quebecers was largely unknown in the anglophone theological milieu of North America. That is why I asked to teach a course on the subject.

In preparation for this course I picked up a book I had bought years ago, but had never read, *Une foi partagée* by Fernand Dumont. The book made a great impression on me. I knew who this author was. He had been appointed by the Quebec bishops in 1968 to chair the Commission on the Laity and the Church, later called the Dumont Commission, whose task was to listen to the spiritual aspirations of the Quebec people and propose pastoral policies in support of a Catholicism appropriate for their society. In the 1980s, Fernand Dumont, by that time an admired sociologist at

Laval University, decided to acquire a doctorate in theology
at his own university. I was invited to become one of the ex-
aminers of his dissertation, yet because his approach to the
theology was so different from the theology with which I was
acquainted, I failed to discover the originality of Dumont's
work. When I read *Une foi partagée* in 2011, I instantly realized that the author was a great theologian, an original thinker, a courageous Christian philosopher ready to face the
challenges modernity poses to the Christian faith. I was now
eager to reread his doctoral dissertation, published in 1987 as
the book *L'institution de la théologie.*

Studying this volume was an arduous adventure. Dumont
is a phenomenologist whose major philosophical work has
been the epistemological presuppositions of the social sciences. As an original thinker he has created his own categories
for understanding the evolution of culture and especially the
production of knowledge. Because he brings his philosophical
approach to the study of the production of theology, his book
is difficult to read, especially for a theologian such as myself
who has had no training in phenomenology. But the effort I
made was a joyful experience. I marvelled at Dumont's familiarity with the philosophers of the West, with the major works
of sociologists and psychologists, and with the literature produced by Christian thinkers from antiquity to modern times.
In interpreting Dumont's thought I was aided by conversa-
tions with two scholars, Serge Cantin and Martin Meunier.
Because Dumont's elevated prose is highly complex and not
always transparent, I offer quotations from his work in free
translation, interpreting his meaning. Yet while *L'institution
de la théologie* appears to be highly theoretical, it is in fact
concerned with the practical issue of daily life in a culture
that continues to change.

In Quebec, Fernand Dumont is honoured as an original
thinker and a public intellectual whose scholarly work is not
confined to a single discipline. He was a sociologist who produced social analyses based on empirical research;[1] he was a

phenomenologist who studied the underlying presuppositions of the social sciences;[2] he often referred to his work as anthropology because in his research he sought to protect the *humanum*;[3] as an historian he interpreted the history of Quebec;[4] as a political scientist he made detailed recommendations for Quebec society;[5] and as a theologian he produced three books.[6] After his death in 1997, his many books were republished as his *Œuvres complètes* in five thick volumes. A year book, *les Cahiers Fernand Dumont*, presents articles that clarify his thought or apply his method to new investigations. His bibliography was published in book form,[7] listing his books, chapters in books, articles, and reviews, as well as the secondary literature, the books, articles, and reviews dealing with his work.

At the same time Dumont was a public figure. He joined the debates over public policies; he published articles in newspapers; he was an ardent supporter of Quebec sovereignty (i.e., its self-constitution as an independent country). For several years he exercised a counselling capacity in the Parti Québécois; in the seventies he promoted a socialism he thought appropriate for the culture of Quebec; and in the nineties he became a vehement critic of the bureaucratized State. Despite his audacious 1964 book on the conversion of Christian thought and the reform of the Church, the Catholic bishops, themselves affected by the Quiet Revolution, put their trust in him when they made him the president of the Commission on the Laity and the Church in 1968. As I mentioned above, the Dumont Report (published 1971) recommended pastoral policies for the future of Quebec Catholicism. While the bishops were unable to adopt these recommendations, they exerted a great influence upon Quebec's theological and pastoral literature.

L'institution de la théologie is a seminal work that could have an important impact on the Catholic Church. It reminded me of John Henry Newman's *An Essay on the Development of Christian Doctrine* (1845). When the study of history in the nineteenth century made unbelievable the Church's claim that its teaching had been identical throughout its history, Newman introduced the idea of doctrinal evolution, a creative process that allowed the Church to develop its teaching while remaining faithful to its original truth. Today, as the Church's credibility is threatened by the secularization of culture, Dumont's book introduces ideas that reveal the relevance and fecundity of the Gospel in the context created by modern society. Yet his book has not yet been received in the Church. The few reviews published in Quebec journals are very positive, but they do not tell the reader what Dumont actually proposes in his work. Nor has it been translated into English or German. In my book *Truth and Relevance: Catholic Theology in French Quebec since the Quiet Revolution*, I promised to write a long essay on *L'institution de la théologie* to introduce its original ideas to an English-speaking readership. I now live up to the promise with some hesitation. There is a philosophical depth in the book that I do not fully grasp. Yet reading the book with my level of understanding offers original ideas that deserve attention and should become part of the theological debate in today's Church.

Before I turn to the study of *L'institution de la théologie* I have to offer a brief description of the Church in Quebec society and present an introduction to some of Dumont's basic socio-philosophical ideas.

QUEBEC SOCIETY AND THE CHURCH

Canada was founded early in the seventeenth century as a colony of France. After the battle of Quebec in 1759 was won by the British forces, France ceded its North American colony to the British Crown in 1763. In response to the firm refusal of the population to abandon its language and its culture, the Quebec Act passed by the British parliament in 1774 allowed the new colony to remain French-speaking, retain its own legal tradition, and stay under the pastoral care of the Catholic

Church. As English-speaking immigrants arrived in British North America in great numbers, first as refugees from the American Revolution, the so-called United Empire Loyalists, and later as settlers coming across the sea from Great Britain, they founded several new colonies. A movement to unite the British North American colonies led in 1867 to the creation of a single country, the Canadian federation, a Dominion in the British Empire, that respected the two linguistic communities and protected their institutions, even as the economic power was in the hands of merchants and industrialists of British origin. The people of Quebec remained faithful to their cultural inheritance. A rebellion in 1836–37 to overcome the province's colonial status and acquire democratic self-government was unsuccessful. In subsequent years, influential leaders, supported by the Catholic Church, persuaded the people of Quebec to resist the Protestant culture of North America, remain farmers and small merchants, be reconciled to their modest situation, and practice the spiritual virtues. The cultural development of the province was the work of the Catholic clergy and the congregations of nuns and brothers: they created and taught in the schools, the colleges, and the universities; they built and staffed hospitals, orphanages, and other institutions serving the common good; they were the social workers who offered help to the poor and to people in difficulties. While the Catholic Church was not formally established as it was in many European countries, the Catholic bishops exerted considerable power: they controlled the culture of the province and influenced the government's public policies. Quebecers accepted this clerical domination largely because a Catholic nation, colonized by an empire of another faith, tends to look upon the Church as a symbol of identity and resistance. This happened in Poland under the Russian Czar, and in Ireland and Quebec under the British Empire.

A rapid cultural change, the so-called Quiet Revolution, began in 1960. The motto of Jean Lesage, the newly elected provincial premier, was 'maîtres chez nous' (masters of our own house). Quebecers rejected the domination of the Anglo elite and decided to live and work in their mother tongue. They demanded freedom of thought, democratic participation, government-sponsored economic development, and a new educational system. They wanted to be a modern society, yet one that respected the values of cooperation and solidarity they had inherited. They called this social democracy or even socialism. This cultural upheaval of the 1960s was accompanied by an intellectual and artistic creativity previously unknown in Quebec history.

The Quiet Revolution was supported by many prominent Catholic personalities. The renewal promoted by Vatican Council II encouraged committed Catholics to advocate a new form of Catholicism, appropriate for the new Quebec, that respected personal freedom and was open to dialogue with the world. The Dominican review *Maintenant* supported this Catholic movement in theological terms and advocated the declericalization of Quebec society.[8] The review insisted that the Church was the believing community and that the mission of the clergy was to help believers to exercise their ministry in church and society, not to become their rulers. Fernand Dumont, an ardent participant in the Quiet Revolution, was part of the Catholic circle close to *Maintenant*. In 1968, responding to the restlessness in the Church, the bishops appointed Fernand Dumont to chair a commission, subsequently called the Dumont Commission, to study the aspirations of the Catholic people and propose pastoral policies for a Catholicism appropriate for the new Quebec.[9] This was a time of great enthusiasm.

Disappointments were not long in coming. In the 1970s, the creative critique of the Church began to become for many an embittered rejection of the Catholic Church. When the report of the Dumont Commission was published in 1971, there was little popular interest in it. At an amazing speed, Quebecers turned their backs on the Church and promoted the secularization of their society. This rapid development has been variously explained by sociologists. As we shall see, Dumont himself has reflected on this phenomenon. Today newspapers and other public media refer to Quebec as a post-Catholic society. Engaged Catholics have become a minority in Quebec; still, they manifest great creativity, inventing innovative pastoral projects, giving courageous testimonies in support of social justice, and producing imaginative explorations of theology.

Disappointing also has been the decline of the social-democratic values that characterized the Quiet Revolution. Quebec has changed under the impact of North American neo liberal capitalism and the domination of instrumental reason produced by the technological imperative. Today the commitment to social solidarity by secular and believing men and women constitutes a movement of resistance representing a minority. The remarkable strike of the students beginning in February 2012 became a movement of social protest, widely supported by Quebecers, reaffirming the ideas and values of the Quiet Revolution.[10]

SOME OF DUMONT'S BASIC IDEAS

Fernand Dumont has repeatedly claimed that his experiences as a child and later as a youth had a powerful impact on his entire philosophical work. Dumont was born in 1927 in Montmorency, a small town near Quebec City, into a modest family belonging to a tightly woven working-class community that had preserved the peasant ethos inherited from its past. Dumont's father worked at the factory of Dominion Textile, owned by English Canadians, where the managers and foremen were anglophones and the workers were obliged to express themselves in their broken English. Dumont admired his parents: despite their poverty, exclusion, and lack of education, they were selfless, generous, and humble, sustained in their difficult lives by their Catholic faith and their Catholic parish. When the young Fernand was sent to school, the teaching brothers soon discovered his outstanding intelligence and his capacity for independent reading. They sent him to better schools and then on to the college curriculum at the seminary, thus making it possible for him to develop his talent and join the community of the educated. Even after he left the environment of his childhood, Dumont remained deeply attached to the values handed on to him by his parents and his parish. He even felt some guilt for having moved beyond the world of his parents. At the same time, a certain restlessness impelled him to intensify his dedication to knowledge and understanding. Later in his philosophy, *rupture* and *fidelity* became important concepts for him. Shortly before he died, he wrote his autobiography, entitling it *The Story of an Emigration*. He still considered himself an emigrant from Montmorency.

Fernand Dumont's central philosophical preoccupation is with culture. Culture communicates to us how we see the world and understand ourselves. "La culture est vision du monde. Elle me fournit un langage, celui d'une communauté historique particulière: elle peuple mon environnement d'objets qui font signe. Elle est ma pré-compréhension des choses et de moi-même."[11] Dumont introduces the distinction between *first* and *second culture*, an invention of his own, that he uses throughout his work dealing with philosophical anthropology. First culture is the taken-for-granted world communicated to children by society through family, school, and the mass media. The first culture mediates a certain memory of the past and a set of values for daily life. While the first culture is inherited, the second culture is constructed. It is the work of human creativity, produced by people performing certain tasks or wrestling with difficult circumstances. Because obstacles, finitude, and contradictions are experienced universally, first cultures are vulnerable: they break open at times – Dumont calls this *le dédoublement* or splitting – and they then provide the energy for the production of the second culture. Our author repeatedly insists that if people want their second culture to thrive and develop, they must remain in touch with the memory and values of the first culture, their cultural inheritance.

Let me apply this distinction to Dumont's early experience. He tells us that his father and mother were non-political: they had been taught to think that their social condition was providential, that it corresponded to the way the world was made, and that it had to be accepted with patience. This was their first culture. Yet Dumont remembers that one time, when he and his father were standing in front of the house in which they lived, they saw a man with a wagon putting the harness on his horses. This made his father say, "They do this to us; they put the harness on our shoulders on Monday morning and take it off on Saturday evening." He felt at that moment that the way he had been forced to live was at odds with the values he had inherited. This was a moment of cultural *dé-doublement*. If the father had pursued this insight with other workers, used his reason to critique their taken-for-granted world, and imagined alternative social relations, he would have helped to construct a second culture. In this process his understanding of himself and his world would have changed. I have invented this imaginative story to illustrate ideas that play an important role in Dumont's thought: he attaches great importance to expressing one's experience, giving witness to it in public, and using reason to explore its implications and engage in action.

Dumont applies the distinction between first and second culture to the different levels of the human efforts to construct society. The first culture provides memory, vitality, and hope, and the second culture is the imaginative work of reason, projecting a new horizon and a new self-understanding. Since every culture is vulnerable to splitting open, people are always in-between; their creativity leads them to experience their finitude and at the same time their desire to transcend it. In Dumont's anthropology, the human being is not a stable substance; he or she is inhabited by an internal dynamics, an experiential tension that produces restlessness and demands creative resolutions. Because humans can never fully know who they are, they are aware of their finitude and at the same time attracted to a depth and meaning that transcends their reason. In his philosophical work, Dumont calls this infinity beyond reach the Transcendence without a name. A religious person interprets this Transcendence as God. This is a topic to which we shall return.

The paradigm of first and second culture plays an important role in Dumont's philosophical and theological thought. It shed light on his own experience. Dumont, an independent intellectual critical of his society, remained committed to the faith and the virtues of his family and their working-class world. The memory of his father and mother, dedicated, faithful, and generous, sustained him in his bold intellectual pursuits.

Great respect for the first culture is not, in my opinion, a universal experience. In his *Modern Social Imaginaries* Charles Taylor points to the ambiguities of the first culture. He argues that the pre-reflective cultural self-understanding in which people grow up inevitably contains some lies and fables that disguise the truth about their society.[12] He does not reduce the entire inherited culture to an ideology; he acknowledges the validity of many of its values and the effort of individuals to live up to them. Dumont himself does not deny the ambiguity of the first culture, even if he chooses to emphasize its resourcefulness. In his own term, the first culture is vulnerable to *le dédoublement* or splitting in response to historical obstacles.

Culture is prior to knowledge. The culture mediated by the institutions to which we belong, Dumont argues, imparts to us a set of values and provides us with a perspective on the world. He writes, "What is culture if not the meaning given to the universe by human beings in order to live together in community, define the norms of acting and knowing, and together interpret their history?"[13] Prior to knowledge, Dumont insists, is an orientation toward reality we have received and embraced. We hold these values and see the world in this light, even though we have no proof for them. We take these values for granted; they are part of our consciousness. We believe them, Dumont likes to insist. Believing, *le croire*, is always prior to knowledge, whether it be the knowledge of common sense or scientific and philosophical concepts. Dumont's major philosophical work has been the critical analysis of the believing, *le croire*, operative in the social sciences and philosophy at various times and in various places. Because the sciences presuppose a believing, their internal structure, he argues, is similar to that of theology, which also assumes a faith. Theology is, therefore, not an anomaly among academic disciplines: all of them rely on reason to examine and explore reality in the light of a particular belief.

If knowledge is dependent on culture, does this imply a relativism of truth? Since cultures not only are diverse but also split open (*le dédoublement*) and change, is it possible to defend the existence of universal truths and values? These are questions with which every sociology of knowledge must wrestle. I had occasion many years ago to study the German social thinkers, Ernst Troeltsch, Max Scheler, and Karl Mannheim: they were convinced of the contextuality of human knowledge, yet they firmly rejected the relativism spreading through the German universities in the first part of the twentieth century. For all of them, in one way or another, the emergence of common truth and values depended upon the commitment of people to a culture of universal solidarity. Troeltsch called this "transcending history by history."[14] We shall see in chapter 5 how Dumont overcomes cultural relativism.

Dumont had an original approach to believing; he also had his own idea of human reason. Using the image of a house with several levels, he recognizes three different functions of human intelligence. On *the ground floor* is the reason we use every day in living our lives, relating to others in the family and at work, and acting responsibly in society. On *the first floor* occurs the formal reason employed in the sciences, applying a logic of mathematical clarity and cognitional procedures seeking truths that are universally recognized. In *the basement* is the reason that continually asks critical questions, raises doubts about the taken-for-granted world, challenges the values and institutions of society, and even interrogates the validity of the sciences. For Dumont, as we saw above, humans are essentially restless: they are torn between their culture and its *dédoublement*. They are driven by reason to question their certitude and engage in the endless pursuit of truth.

For Dumont, reason in the basement is not metaphysical; it is not an echo of Platonic or Aristotelian reason. As a phenomenologist, the Quebec philosopher analyzes reason by closely observing human experience. He shows that in people's lives, reason eventually raises questions for which the finite world has no answer; yet instead of resigning itself to this ultimate ignorance, reason reaches impatiently, yet unsuccessfully, to the Infinite. As we saw above, Dumont holds that the experience of finitude and the desire to transcend it reveal the presence of an Absolute, a nameless Transcendence, which religious people designate as God.

Introducing Dumont's basic ideas, I have mentioned three of them: his distinction between first and second culture, the primacy he assigns to believing, and the threefold understanding of human intelligence. I wish to add to this Dumont's creative idea of the imagination.

In the Catholic theological tradition, the imagination has a low cognitive status. According to scholastic philosophy, the making of images always accompanies rational thinking, yet these images are inferior to the rational concepts. Images can be made of things that do not exist and even of things that cannot exist, such as a mermaid with the tail of a fish. The scholastics did not recognize that images can be bearers of meaning that transcend conceptualization. They acknowledged the power of the sacraments, which are images or signs, yet they were unaware that God's Word is mediated to humans by images. In the Scriptures and the liturgy, the images and rituals that communicate divine revelation are always accompanied by a word or a message that assures their correct interpretation. To avoid misunderstanding the images of divine revelation, the Church has increasingly nailed down their meaning in clearly defined concepts. While doctrines may fulfill a useful role, Dumont repeatedly warns theologians and pastors not to look upon divine revelation as a series of ideas to be believed. As we shall see further on, our author holds that biblical revelation occurs in stories which appeal to the imagination and address ever new messages to the believing community.

Dumont draws his own idea of the imagination from the French phenomenologist Gaston Bachelard, who looked upon the imaginative capacity of the mind as a power greater than reason.[15] Reason is reasonable, predictable, in control, and proud of its achievements, yet there is more to the human mind. Within it can be awakened a source of creativity that produces ever new dreams, images, ideals, and illusions – in other words, an imagination, capable of stopping reason from saying No and from staying within its self-created boundaries.

Dumont recalls that new inventions and new ideas in the sciences have always been prepared by imagining the new, long before it was realizable by the power of reason. Humans dreamt of flying in the air long before they invented the airplane, and hypotheses in mathematics and theoretical physics are the work of the imagination to be subsequently tested by reason. As we shall see, in order to make the Church more truly evangelical, Dumont makes imaginative proposals for ecclesiastical reform that seem unrealizable at present, yet they stimulate the mind, encourage pastoral experiments, and foster a new way of seeing the Church, making reforms feasible in the future. Implicit in Dumont's understanding of the imagination is the recognition of the role of utopia in the making of human history. In his *La vigile du Québec* he presents his own commitment to socialism as utopian. He writes, "Jamais nos sociétés contemporaines n'auront eu tant besoin de l'utopie."[16]

L'INSTITUTION DE LA THÉOLOGIE

The title of the book *L'institution de la théologie* is unclear in French and incomprehensible when translated into English. Sociologists, it should be remembered, regard all cultural expressions as instituted. Human language with its syntax and grammar is an institution. Language is a social product allowing people to be in conversation, constitute a community, and cooperate in providing the goods they need for survival. Language is accompanied by instituted rites and symbols that allow people to remember their origin, be confirmed in their present tasks, and express their collective hope for the future. Society is instituted; and within society science, philosophy, and theology are instituted, inevitably reflecting in some way the society that supports them.

Dumont's major work has been on the institution of the social sciences and philosophy. He has examined how the institutional conditions of scientific and philosophical inquiry affect the knowledge they produce. He has also studied how the institution of the professions, such as medical doctors and educators, influences their self-understanding and their practice. His entire scholarly work can be interpreted as a series of studies in the sociology of knowledge. Our author recognizes that the production of knowledge is always contextual: it takes place under certain circumstances and relies on presuppositions drawn from its cultural environment. At the same time, the sociology of knowledge does not imply that intellectuals are completely determined by their context and thus inevitably conformist. On the contrary, for our author, true intellectuals are critics of their society.

Dumont believes that intellectuals have a high calling: they are destined to raise the critical questions that society prefers to overlook. "À l'intellectuel semble alors revenir cette tâche extraordinaire: définir, pour la communauté des hommes, non pas seulement de nouveaux objectifs et de nouvelles valeurs, mais la société elle-même."[17] In this, intellectuals differ from specialists who remain within their own discipline and think that their approach to knowledge is objective and essentially unrelated to society. Because they have an impact on the social order, intellectuals are exposed to many pressures.[18] If they are dependent upon the authorities or simply rely on scientific research, they may find it impossible to live up to their calling, which is to deal critically with the values and ideals of their society. If they have embraced the dominant culture, they will be unable to fulfill their task. Intellectuals, Dumont holds, find themselves in a conflictive situation. Their malaise becomes deeply troubling if they are torn apart between their commitment to truth and the constraints put on them by society. Every true intellectual is in one way or another an emigrant, and as such, ill at ease and at odds with his or her world. Our author, we recall, entitled his autobiography *Récit d'une émigration*. Rupture, Dumont insists, is the starting point of all new ideas. The intellectual must risk standing alone, as the specialist and expert need not.

In *L'institution de la théologie* Dumont looks upon the theologian as an intellectual, a critical thinker in the believing community. Theologians differ from religious philosophers because their faith inserts them in the community of believers, to which they are related in various ways and which makes certain demands on them. Our author calls these relations *ruptures*: they are obligatory signposts that interrupt the free thinking of the person in search of the truth. In exploring the Christian faith, theology is thus instituted in a unique manner, linked as it is to the Church by this very faith. While Dumont developed his methodological approach in dialogue with the secular sciences, his *L'institution de la théologie* is a properly theological work. He studies the role and the task of the theologian, not as a secular scholar looking at the Church from the outside – in itself a legitimate undertaking – but as a believing Catholic, looking upon the Church, its origin and its history, with the eyes of faith.

Because *L'institution de la théologie* is a work of theology, it has been overlooked by philosophers and social thinkers who are familiar with Dumont's phenomenological methodology yet who do not share his Catholic faith. At the same time, theologians unacquainted with Dumont's philosophical method have found *L'institution de la théologie* a difficult book to understand. This is the reason, I think, why the innovative thought of Dumont has not yet been received in Quebec's theological milieu. Yet it would be an error to think of Dumont as a remote, academic thinker unconcerned about the aspirations and sorrows of ordinary people. We shall see that for our author the purpose of theological inquiries is the enhancement of the daily lives of believers, offering guidance for responding creatively to their cultural context.

The task of the theologian is not simply to study the revealed truths in the Scriptures, clarify their meaning, and achieve a better understanding of the Christian faith. Nor is the theologian a thinker identified with the ecclesiastical institution, providing an interpretation of Christian faith that legitimizes the organizational concerns of the Church's hierarchy. In five long chapters, Dumont shows how the theologian responds to the signposts provided by his or her faith, or, in Dumont's language, how the faith constitutes the theological enterprise. Chapter 2 of *L'institution de la théologie* develops the relation of theology to the believing community, chapter 3 clarifies the relation of theology to the magisterium, chapter 4 examines theology's dependence on Scripture and the tradition of faith, chapter 5 shows that theology includes a critical evaluation of the culture to which it belongs, and chapter 6 proposes in what directions theology must move at the present time.

I shall review chapters 2 to 6 of *L'institution de la théologie* in chapters 2 to 6 of this book. The text of *L'institution* from which I quote is published in *Œuvres complètes de Fernand Dumont* (Quebec: PUL, 2008), volume 4, 149–408.

The Theologian and the Community of Believers

In and for the community of believers, theologians think and speak as mediators. Mediation is a category of great importance for Dumont. He never forgets that our entry into personhood takes place through the mediation offered by parents, family, school, and culture. To recognize in what ways theologians are mediators in and for the believing community, we have to understand what Dumont means by Christian faith.

THE FAITH EXPERIENCE

The person who has faith is addressed by a message of new life, surrenders to it, and responds to it by reorienting his or her life. Faith takes place in the mind, touches the heart, and finds expression in witnessing action. Faith in the Gospel changes people's lives, summons them to create a community, and calls them to a solidarity that has no boundaries. According to our author, the Church is alive, resourceful, and capable of renewing itself, thanks to the faith experience of the believing community. The vitality of this community is not produced by priests, bishops, or popes: it is generated by religious experience and sustained by the life of faith. The Church's creativity is generated by the Spirit in the minds and hearts of the faithful.

Experience has two meanings for our author. To "have an experience" refers to a particular event that affects one's life in a manner one cannot forget; and to "have experience" refers to the knowledge or wisdom acquired through familiarity with certain conditions. The faith of the Christian, the Spirit-given foundation of the Church, deserves to be called "experience" in this twofold sense: it refers to particular moments when believers are addressed by God's Word and to the wisdom they have acquired through familiarity with the Scriptures and the life of the Church.

The experience of faith is one thing; its expression is another. The experience urges people to speak about it, communicate it to others, and give witness to it in public life. But the expression they choose is unable to communicate it in its richness, depth, and fertility. In Dumont's anthropology of human knowing developed in his major publications, the distance between experience and its expression plays an important role. This distance belongs to the dissatisfaction that is part of the human condition. That no expression is capable of exhausting the meaning of an experience is frustrating and, at the same time, the springboard for new thought, searching out ideas that express the as-yet-overlooked depth and richness of the experience. We shall see further on that for our author there are several tensions in the makeup of human beings that produce an internal dynamics of thinking and acting. The distance between experience and its expression is one of them.

In many situations, Catholics express their faith in the recognized discourse of the Church. That their Christian experience does not completely correspond to the expression of Christian truth in the sermons of their parish priest does not bother them a great deal. Yet in times of major cultural transformation, people, including Christian people, change: they see the world and themselves in a new light, and their religious experiences no longer correspond to the dominant discourse in the Church. In this situation, the theologian serves the believing community as mediator, helping believers to express their religious experience. The theologian will listen to them, take their experience seriously, and propose to them formulations that reveal the rootedness of their experience in Scripture and Tradition.

Dumont admires the creative power of Christian faith in the Christian communities of Africa and Latin America. The ecclesiastical authorities sometimes judge new movements as unorthodox and try to suppress them, a pastoral response that Dumont finds regrettable. By crushing religious fervour and imposing orthodox doctrine, the authorities may be squashing the vitality which is the source of the Church's power. The theologian acting as mediator will listen carefully to the new religious experience and help the believing community find an expression of its experience that reveals its link to the Scriptures and its rootedness in the Catholic tradition. The theologian may be able to mediate the passage from the first to the second religious culture in a manner that protects the authenticity of the Catholic tradition.

Our author suggests that the rapid spread of Christianity in Africa may be due to its power to act as mediator, allowing believers to be reconciled to the modernity that invades their country and at the same time feel at home in the cultural world of Jesus that resembles their own African inheritance. Dumont also praised the Latin American bishops and their theologians at the Medellin Conference of 1968 for listening to the religious experience of the creative movements in the Church and formulating expressions of this experience that reveal its dependence on aspects of Scripture and Tradition that have been largely overlooked in the past. Significant also is the rapid spread of Evangelical and Pentecostal Christianity in Latin America, the Philippines, and certain regions of Africa. Dumont suggests that this type of Christianity acts as mediator, helping believers to become self-reliant personalities, industrious workers, and respectful of their wives, and at the same time providing ecstatic forms of worship that re-awaken tribal memories. Our author's suggestions are simply hypotheses; he recognizes the need for careful empirical research.

Dumont does not mention in this chapter that he had been appointed by the Quebec bishops in 1968 to chair a commission charged with producing a report on the status and role of the laity in the Church, subsequently called the Dumont Report.[1] The commission held hearings in the various parts of Quebec and invited Catholics and Catholic institutions to submit briefs expressing their religious aspirations. Dumont thought that after the upheaval produced by the Quiet Revolution, the Church of Quebec would be renewed and revitalized by the faith experiences of the believing community. Listening to laypersons, the commission tried to express their spiritual aspirations in a manner that revealed their newness and at the same time their fidelity to the Catholic inheritance. The Second Vatican Council had encouraged this bold theological undertaking: it had asked theologians to enter into dialogue with the culture to which they belonged and learn to express the Gospel in terms that could be understood in their cultural context.[2] The Council said specifically, "Indeed, accommodated preaching of the revealed Word ought to remain the law of all evangelization. For thus the ability to express Christ's message in its own way is developed in each nation."[3] In each nation, the truth of the Gospel is to be proclaimed in a contextual manner, attentive to the culture, the problems, and the aspirations of the people. In the years after the Council, the bishops and theologians of Quebec, including Fernand Dumont, took this recommendation with utmost seriousness. They wanted to create a Catholicism that corresponded to the faith experience of the Quebec people.

In the Quiet Revolution, Quebec society joined other Western industrial societies by embracing modern culture, which was marked by both humanizing and dehumanizing trends. Particular to Quebec was the national drama: a people with a cultural history of its own was now a province of a country that defined its identity in very different terms. Still, Quebec Catholics shared with other Western Christians the believing encounter with modernity. In the pages that follow, I wish to look at this encounter. By examining three religious experiences I wish to illustrate Fernand Dumont's thesis: first, that the vitality of the Church resides in the faith-experience of the baptized, and second, that theologians act as mediators helping the former to express their experience in keeping with the Catholic tradition.

THREE NEW RELIGIOUS EXPERIENCES

The analysis of the following three religious experiences is implicitly contained in *L'institution de la théologie*, yet their description and exploration are my own.

The Call to Historical Co-responsibility

Democracies expect their citizens to be co-responsible for their society. In this situation, Christians come to feel that this co-responsibility is part of their spiritual identity. To be a citizen is for them an ethical task. In the vocabulary used by John Paul II, human beings are "subjects,"[4] responsible agents accountable for their own lives and answerable with others for the institutions to which they belong. In his encyclical *Sollicitudo Rei Socialis* (1987) he advocates "the creative subjectivity of citizens" and laments that some nations are still deprived of "their subjectivity."

Since the Quiet Revolution persuaded and convinced Quebecers that they were "subjects," the Dumont Report recommended that the Church recognize them as actors co-responsible for their society as well as for their Church. Since they experience themselves as subjects, the baptized want to say their words and be heard in the believing community. The absence of institutions facilitating dialogue between the baptized and the ecclesiastical authorities reveals that the hierarchy has not yet responded to the believers' new self-understanding as subjects. The creation of such institutions is an urgent recommendation of the Dumont Report.

The human as "subject" is a theme developed by the personalist philosophy of Emmanuel Mounier († 1950). This French philosopher and his circle of friends were critical of the liberalism dominant in the English-speaking world, seeing that it fostered individualism and had no concept of the common good. Mounier and his friends were also critical of the communism produced in the Soviet Union, seeing that it fostered collectivism that did not respect the freedom of individuals. What Mounier proposed was a middle way, which he called *personalism*, that understood persons, not as severed individuals, but as rooted in community, responsible for community, and in solidarity with the entire human family. The personalist philosophy, embraced in his own way by Jacques Maritain, exerted great influence in the Catholic world, including Quebec.[5] It subsequently found expression in the documents of the Second Vatican Council and the writings of Pope John Paul II.

Fernand Dumont knew the work of Emmanuel Mounier, regarded him as an important Christian thinker and witness, and fully shared his conviction that in modern society human beings are accountable agents responsible for their personal and institutional lives.[6] Yet according to our author, it was not the personalist philosophy that had brought forth this new self-understanding. New ideas and new ideals emerge as people struggle to overcome the obstacles that diminish their lives. The entry into the second culture, we recall, is a response to the split experience (*le dédoublement*) in the first culture. A dramatic experience in the societies of the West has been the struggle for citizenship – that is to say, for a society that recognizes its members as co-responsible for the common good. Traditional society had been hierarchical, made up of *maiores* and *minores*, the former being men with power and

authority and the latter the people obliged to obey them. Here
the few decided what should happen to the many without
asking them. The Catholic Church adopted this system of
governance. The struggle for co-responsibility and participation took centuries and has not as yet been completed. But the
discourse of democracy and the frustration over its imperfect
practice have produced, in people on every level of society, the
desire to become vocal and active participants therein. People
no longer think of themselves as subjects of a prince, committed to loyalty and obedience; they now see themselves as responsible agents, as "subjects" in a different sense. They do
not want to be "objects" maneuvered by the decrees of the
ruler; they want to be "subjects," co-creators of the laws that
order their societies and institutions. This struggle has produced a new personal self-understanding; personalist philosophy has subsequently clarified, blessed, and legitimized it.

The theologian as mediator helps the Catholic people to
find an appropriate expression of their experience. That
human beings are to be the subjects of their history is as such
not revealed in the Scriptures: the books of the Old and New
Testaments reflect the societal imagination of the times. Yet
listening to the biblical summons for personal responsibility
in a modern society reveals people's vocation to become the
authors and artisans of their collective existence. The Second
Vatican Council acknowledged this in this oft-cited sentence:
"We are witnesses of the birth of a new humanism, one in
which man is defined first of all by this responsibility to his
brothers (and sisters) and to history."[7] Lifting this sentence
out of its context in *Gaudium et Spes*, it could be read as a
confession of human autonomy independent of God. Needless
to say, this is not what the sentence means. Interpreting people's responsibility for themselves and their world as a secular
faith does not correspond to the experience of the believing
community. Believers experience their autonomy as sustained
by God's grace, and perceive the social concern urging them
to become actors in history as a gift of the Holy Spirit. Let me

add that Dumont recognizes God's presence in man's making of man even in his secular scientific works.

Quebec theologians always do their thinking against the background of the rapid secularization of their society. We shall see that Dumont has much to say on this topic. One point that he has repeatedly made is that the organization of the Catholic Church no longer corresponds to the self-understanding of the Catholic people. They want to be "subjects" of the Church. The papal-episcopal system inherited by the Church, Dumont argues, does not in principle prohibit the creation of institutions for dialogue and co-responsibility. In fact, impressed by the fertility of dialogue at the Second Vatican Council, Paul VI wrote the encyclical *Ecclesiam Suam* (1964) proposing that dialogue *ad intra* and *ad extra* be the way of the Church in the future. Unfortunately Paul VI did not keep his promise when he published the encyclical *Humanae Vitae* (1968), condemning the use of birth control, without consulting even the bishops, let alone married couples in the Church.

In her book *The Roman Catholic Clerical Exodus*, the sociologist Janice Newson shed light on this unresolved problem in the Church.[8] She interviewed a large number of Catholic priests in the Toronto area who had left the priesthood and an equal number of priests in the same area who had remained in the priesthood. Her purpose was to find the reasons why so many priests had left the priesthood in the years following the Second Vatican Council. I read her conclusion over thirty-five years ago and have never forgotten it. Janice Newson showed that the Vatican Council had introduced a new discourse in the Church, recognizing the need for dialogue, consultation, and participation, yet had not changed the institutions that continued to operate in the traditional authoritarian manner. It was the frustration over the disconnection between the discourse and the institution, Janice Newson argued, that convinced a large number of priests to resign from their ministry. Newson's analysis corresponds to an observation repeatedly made by Fernand Dumont: if the Church does not respond creatively to the culture in which it finds itself, it will be experienced by people as a foreign body, unrelated to their real concerns.

Let me add at this point that Dumont rarely mentions that over the last two decades a growing number of conservative Catholics, encouraged by the Vatican, have stressed the supreme authority of the pope and resisted the intra-ecclesial dialogue recommended by the Second Vatican Council. It is interesting that these conservative Catholics have become actors in the Church, have formed groups and institutes to promote their ideas, and try to influence bishops, episcopal conferences, and the congregations of the Vatican. They too, despite their theory, see themselves as subjects of the Church. In our culture, this experience is inescapable.

The Conversion to God's Redemptive Immanence

In modern society, people come to understand themselves as subjects of their history, and Christians see their co-responsibility for society as their spiritual vocation. This new religious self-understanding was fostered by political events of the twentieth century that challenged Christians to rethink their role in history. We recall that in 1939, when Hitler's army invaded Poland, a Catholic nation, Pius XII did not protest: he still had the traditional belief that major historical events are part of God's inscrutable providence, and that the salvation brought by Jesus Christ deals with the higher order of prayer, holiness, and eternal life. The same theological understanding persuaded the German bishops during World War II not to condemn the genocides perpetrated by their government. The Barmen Declaration of the Protestant Confessing Church offered a different reading of the Gospel. "As Jesus Christ is God's comforting pronouncement of the forgiveness of all our sins, so, with equal seriousness, he is also God's vigorous announcement of his claim upon our whole life." The message of salvation affects the whole of life, including our role in society and our political engagement. After the war, Christians in all the Churches became convinced that God's Word summoned them to become responsible actors in history.

A similar religious experience occurred after World War II during the struggles of the colonized peoples of Africa and Asia for political self-determination. The Churches now realized that in the exercise of their mission, they had been on the side of the colonizers, accepting their protection, a bitter discovery that led to their conversion. They now asked for forgiveness and expressed their solidarity with the peoples struggling to define their future. What the Churches failed to realize before was that fidelity to the Gospel demands a critical understanding of one's place in history.

The Good News preached by Jesus to the people in his land dealt with life on Earth, not with heaven. He announced God's coming reign. "Thy kingdom come," he prayed, adding, "thy will be done on earth, as it is in heaven." If the Christian vocation is to do God's will on Earth and assume co-responsibility for history, the message dealing with the salvation of souls loses its place at the centre of attention, and in fact distracts believers from their essential task of doing God's will on Earth. Many Christians in modern society have been impressed by this earthly reading of the Gospel. They find it increasingly difficult to think of God in heaven, the all-powerful king of the universe, who rules human history from above. The traditional theism has become problematic to them. This unsettling experience is described in a brief encounter imaged by the French philosopher Maurice Blondel, writing at the end of the nineteenth century. He wrote that if an angel came into his room with a message from a higher world, he would refuse to listen to it, claiming that his divine vocation, his "*métier d'homme*," was to act responsibly in the present world. Blondel rejected what he called "supernaturalism." A message, even of divine origin, is only credible, he argued, if it responds in some way to the questions that trouble people's minds and disturb their hearts. A divine message is believable only if it is relevant to people's effort to transcend their present situation and fulfill their human vocation. For many believers in modern society, the God of the Bible is no longer imagined as a supreme being above history, ruling the world from his heavenly throne; instead, God now appears to them as a personal presence in history, summoning and empowering humans to be faithful to their vocation. This position of God as a personal presence in history, often referred to as panentheism, has been adopted in one way or another by a great number of Christian theologians, including Fernand Dumont.

Blondel produced a phenomenology of human existence according to which an inner dynamics carried humans forward to realize themselves through ever wider ranges of solidarity and an openness to the unknowable Infinite. As a Christian, Blondel believed that this Transcendence present as summons in people's lives was the God revealed in the Scriptures. God is here the gracious dimension of man's making of man. Blondel's panentheism did not predict the inevitable progress of civilization; instead, God's redemptive immanence assured a summons to an endless conversion to greater love.

Dumont does not follow Blondel's phenomenology of human becoming, yet he does share Blondel's conviction that operative within the human person is an internal dynamics that makes them restless, respond creatively to obstacles, emigrate from the first to a second culture, and increasingly makes them forget themselves in the love of another. We already referred to one aspect of this dynamics: the fact that the experience is never fully articulated in its expression. Dumont shows that human beings constantly confront their finitude, even though they yearn to transcend this limitation. They are never fully at home with themselves because they are unable to live up to their spiritual calling. Present in their lives, Dumont argues, is a Transcendence without a name.

Is this Transcendence just an idea that haunts us or does it have reality? A philosopher may not be able to reply to this question. Dumont refers to the atheist philosopher Max Horkheimer, the founder of the Frankfurt School, who toward the end of his life wrote the book *Die Sehnsucht nach dem ganz Anderen*,[9] which confesses a nameless Transcendence in human life that may be unreal – yet longing for it is the unique foundation of an ethics of love and justice. I came across a quotation from Albert Camus that acknowledges an internal dynamics in human life that carries humanity forward in an ongoing quest of creativity, which he interprets as an unbeliever.

> That man is the only creature that refuses to be what
> he is, means that the human dimension – his grandeur
> and dignity, including the achievements of science, the arts
> and human love – arises from his own choice, in an end-
> less search to become ever more the creator of himself
> and his world, committed to this quest that becomes
> ever more human with him.[10]

Fernand Dumont held that the nameless Transcendence that humans encounter in the changing situations of their lives is the God revealed in the Scriptures. Many Quebec theologians share this conviction. According to Dumont's analysis, human life has a religious dimension. His argument, we notice, is not metaphysical: he does not share the position of the older Catholic tradition that reason, following the lead of Plato or Aristotle, can demonstrate the existence of a Supreme Being. Dumont is a phenomenologist convinced that an in-depth de-scription of human experience is able to show that present in human life are moments of encounter with the Infinite, un-knowable though it be. Dumont shared this conviction with Blondel. Even Blondel's atheist contemporary, the sociologist Émile Durkheim, produced a phenomenology of society, per-suading him that "there was something eternal in religion."[11] Dumont himself did not think that the secularization of

Quebec society and the growing indifference to religion in the
Western world would make religion disappear: it would simply come to manifest itself in new ways.

A DIFFERENT PERSPECTIVE

I wish to mention in this context that my own discovery of
Maurice Blondel's thought in the late 1960s produced in me
something like an intellectual conversion: I was greatly impressed by his passage from traditional theism to panentheism. This passage, I was convinced, corresponded to the
experience of vast numbers of Christians in the modern age.
At the same time, I was not persuaded by Blondel's description
of the internal dynamics that carried humans to the encounter
with the Infinite. His account failed to convince me – as does
Dumont's – because I have good friends committed to doing
good who are thoroughly secular with no inkling of an
Absolute. I was unable to accept that religion was a constitutive dimension of human existence. In my book *Man Becoming*
(1970),[12] I presented a version of panentheism that did not
imply that humans were moved by a logic internal to them to
encounter Transcendence. In dialogue with the Scriptures, ex-
istentialism, and psychotherapy, I argued that God was gratu-
itously present in human life as Word and as Spirit: the Word
summoning us through many voices to come to self-knowl-
edge, repent, and love our neighbour, and the Spirit enabling
us through many associations to become responsible actors in
the world. Thanks to God's unmerited presence in their lives,
people are rescued from their self-destructive potential, their
egotism, and their fears, and discover within themselves the
power to act, promote peace, struggle for justice, and opt for
solidarity with the poor and excluded. The message of Jesus
reveals to us God's redemptive presence in human history
from the beginning. Because of the brokenness into which
humans are born, one can say that God is the redemptive
Mystery that makes humanity possible.

My theological proposal does not suppose a built-in orientation in human beings towards an encounter with the Divine.

As a result of my own experiences, which differ from those of Dumont, God is always rescuer or redeemer, saving us unexpectedly from our self-destructive potentials and protecting us from harm. I prefer to think that God, out of pure love, addresses people, lifts them up, and gives them the freedom to do good. Some people acknowledge this divine summons and become believers, while there are others who simply do God's will: they practice love, justice, and peace while remaining wholly secular. The New Testament seems to recognize that the lives of secular people may be touched by God's grace. In a famous parable, Jesus acknowledges that whatever people do for the poor, "the least of the brethren" (Mt 25:40), they actually do for him, the Christ, even if they do not know him nor have ever heard of him.

Let me add that I have sympathy for thoughtful persons who tell me that they are unable to believe in God because of the endless misery inflicted upon people in this world. Because their unbelief is based on solidarity with the victims of history, I refer to it as theological atheism and I don't think that God is displeased with it.

The two versions of panentheism, Dumont's and my own, are at odds with the statement often made by churchmen that the significant division of humanity is between believers and non-believers – the Church against the world. In his encyclical *Caritas in Veritate* (2009), Benedict XVI argues that the most urgent need in today's troubled world is the conversion to God and that "a humanism that excludes God is an inhuman humanism."[13] More persuasive is the thesis of panentheism that the significant division of humanity is between humans committed to truth, love, and justice and humans captured in personal and collective selfishness.

The Reconciliation with Religious Pluralism

I have mentioned two experiences common in modern society that have affected Christian self-understanding: the call to historical co-responsibility and the conversion to God's

redemptive immanence. A third challenging experience has
been the response to the religious pluralism of modern society. In traditional societies, the inherited religion provided the
coordinates for interpreting society and the cosmos, relegat-
ing the followers of other religions to the dark regions of
god-forsakenness. Christians avoided contact with heretics,
Jews, and pagans. The religious pluralism of modern society,
intensified in recent decades by waves of new immigrants, has
made the association with "others" a daily occurrence affect-
ing the self-understanding of Christians. Unless they opt for a
rigid sectarianism, Christians come to admit that the God in
whom they believe transcends the Christian Church and sustains the lives of men and women in other faith traditions.
The Church's proclamation of the Gospel no longer implies
that there is no truth outside the Church. What has emerged
is an experience of universal solidarity, acknowledged at the
Second Vatican Council in the opening lines of *Gaudium et
Spes.* "The joys and the hopes, the griefs and the anxieties of
the men (and women) of this age, especially those who are
poor or in any way afflicted, these are the joys and hopes, the
griefs and anxieties of the followers of Christ."

The experience of solidarity in God with the followers of
other religions has been a disturbing event because it ap-
peared to contradict biblical teaching. I found it interesting
that Farid Esack, a Muslim theologian from South Africa, has
described a similar disturbing experience within the faith of
Islam. His family's troubled life under the apartheid regime
was made bearable, he tells us, thanks to the solidarity and
the sense of humour of their Christian neighbours. He writes,
"How could I have looked into the eyes of Mrs Batista and
Aunt Katie, believing that despite the kindness they showed
my family in so many ways, they were destined to be condemned to hell."[14] This experience made him reread the
Koran and rethink the Islamic teaching he had received.

How difficult it was for Christians to deal with this new
experience is well documented in the gradual evolution of

Joseph Ratzinger's attitude to religious pluralism. In the Instruction *Dominus Jesus* published in 2000 by the Congregation for the Doctrine of the Faith and signed by Cardinal Ratzinger as its president, we still read that "religious pluralism exists only in fact (de facto), for in principle (de jure) there is only one religion, the Catholic Church."[15] As Pope Benedict XVI, speaking in Regensburg in 2006, he still declared that Christians and Muslims do not worship the same God. In several addresses after that date, Benedict gradually changed his mind, an evolution I have analyzed in detail,[16] right up to his speech at Benin on 19 November 2011, praising Africa's religious and cultural pluralism: "I would like to use the image of a hand," he said. "There are five fingers on it and each one is quite different. Each one is also essential and their unity makes a hand."[17]

Theologians as mediators have paid attention to the new religious experience and examined whether it can be reconciled with Scripture and integrated into the Catholic tradition. This has become an important debate in Catholic theology. A widely accepted proposal has been the retrieval of the ancient Logos-Christology, according to which the Word or Logos that became incarnate in Jesus of Nazareth actually resounds throughout the whole of human history, summoning forth in all wisdom traditions a yearning for the Absolute. This theological proposal was in fact adopted by the Declaration *Nostra Aetate* of the Second Vatican Council to justify the new openness of the Church in regard to the world religions. How theologians show that the new experience has the support of biblical revelation, I shall discuss in chapter 4.

Let me add that the Logos-Christology is not the last word; it is simply a first attempt to honour religious pluralism. Since this theological proposal does not sufficiently acknowledge the differences among the world religions, making them all dependant on the biblical tradition, theologians are looking for alternative interpretations of religious pluralism.

FIRST AND SECOND THEOLOGY

Fernand Dumont presents the theologian as mediator helping believers to reflect on their religious experience, take a critical look at it, and then express it in a manner sustained by the sources of faith – Scripture, Tradition, and the magisterium. As mediator the theologian serves the integrity of the Catholic tradition and the unity of the believing community. What this means concretely, we shall see in the next chapter. Our author calls this commitment "a rupture" because it opts against theologizing as a purely private spiritual adventure. For Dumont, theology is always ecclesial.

Dumont recognizes the need for an academic theology. The ancient dictum *fides quaerens intellectum* (faith in search of understanding) retains its validity and demands that theologians be in dialogue with the secular thought of their own generation. At the same time, he insists that thinking believers who question their faith and seek greater insight are in fact also theologians. Strangely enough, I have not found in *L'institution de la théologie* any reference to the uncertain future of theological faculties in Quebec. Today fewer students choose to become theologians, and as society becomes more secular, fewer public funds will support theological education and research. Yet it is not fear of the decline of academic theology that persuades Dumont to attach great importance to the theological reflection of ordinary believers. This reflection is summoned forth by faith itself.

In present-day society, Christian faith is no longer handed on by cultural inheritance; faith represents a personal option, a believing listening supported by continued reasoning. Therefore all believers actually think theologically. Dumont argues that discussing the questions raised by faith in the parishes has great pastoral importance. While the participants may lack acquaintance with academic theology, they reflect intelligently on their faith experience and produce their own theology. Dumont distinguishes between the "first theology" of ordinary believers and the "second theology" of academically trained theologians. First theology is expressed in the works of many writers and artists. Dumont refers specifically to Dante, Pascal, Péguy, and Bernanos. In Quebec the novels of Jean Bédard[18] provide sophisticated theological reflection. Dumont suggests that this is a field of research that has been largely neglected. He is even willing to recognize as first theology the reflections of non-believers who explore the conflict between the finitude of human life and its yearning for the infinite, or who reflect on the meaning and power of Jesus of Nazareth. In Quebec, Catholics have been edified by the essays of Bernard Émond, who declares himself a non-believer.[19] The exploration of the hidden theological content of literature and works of art is not altogether new. I remember the German theologian Romano Guardini, who, before and after World War II, published studies of Socrates, Hölderlin, Dostoyevsky, Scheler, Rilke, and other thinkers and artists. Dumont's distinction between first and second theology creates a respected space for the theological insights of non-theologians. Accusing German academic theology of being irrelevant, Dorothee Soelle, an original thinker and poet, produced her own theological reflections on the religious experience of her contemporaries. Also critical of academic theology is a recent book by the American Protestant theologian Mark Lewis Taylor, who prefers to study the theological ideas implicit in the writings of contemporary philosophers and novelists who do not regard themselves as orthodox Christians or Jews, but whose reflections on Transcendence deserve attention.[20] Taylor places their thought in the category of "the theological" and predicts that in the future the theological will have a greater impact on society than academic theology.

Dumont, as this book tries to show, has not lost confidence in academic theology as long as it listens to the experience of the believing community and tries to respond to the anguish and the insights of its cultural environment.

Our author's emphasis on the faith of the people as the source of the Church's vitality raises questions which he does not discuss at length. Is the faith of the people trustworthy? Is their common faith not affected by the dominant ideology of society? Is it not true that the common faith needs the prophetic witness to become truly faithful to the Gospel? These questions are asked by Catholics unhappy with the resistance of many believers, including members of the hierarchy, to the renewal initiated by the Second Vatican Council.

It is my impression that Dumont's positive presentation of the people's common faith is related to his participation in the Christian awakening that accompanied the Quiet Revolution. He belonged to the group of intellectuals associated with the Dominican review *Maintenant* and eventually became a member of its editorial committee. This bold review spearheaded a new form of Catholicism appropriate for the new Quebec. A recent book on *Maintenant, Une réforme dans la fidélité*, demonstrates that the bold proposals of the review tried to preserve and enhance the authentic Catholic tradition.[21] Dumont enjoyed this Catholic milieu.[22] His book *Pour la conversion de la pensée chrétienne*, published in 1964, offered radical theological proposals that expressed the spiritual aspirations of the Catholic people. He thought of himself as the mediator, articulating the religious experience of Quebecers as they wrestled to redefine themselves as a modern, autonomous society. In 1968, appointed by the bishops as chair of the study commission on the laity in the Church, known as the Dumont Commission, he held hearings all over the province of Quebec, received hundreds of briefs from Catholic groups and individuals, and after three years produced a report that he and his commission regarded as an accurate expression of the religious aspirations of the great majority of Quebecers. These events and experiences in the 1960s, I believe, persuaded Dumont to trust the common faith of the people and admire its creativity. In later years our author was greatly troubled by the confused religious ideas of the Quebec Catholics who still went to Mass on Sundays.[23]

3

The Theologian and the Magisterium

The task of theologians is mediation. They mediate the spiritual insights and aspirations of the people to the teaching authorities, and they mediate the Church's official teaching to the people by explaining it and showing its foundation in the sources of faith. Still, Dumont recognizes that in many historical situations the relation of theologians to the ecclesiastical magisterium has been a dialectic of distance and loyalty. He illustrates this with references to the theological debates before and during the Second Vatican Council. Theologians who had been critical of the Church's official teaching were invited by the Council to become *periti*, official theologians, helping the bishops to articulate the faith of the Church.

THE MAGISTERIUM IN HISTORY

Our author argues that in opposition to the Protestant Reformation, the Catholic Church presented itself as mother and teacher of the unchanging Christian truth throughout the ages. The Church's magisterium claimed to be *semper idem*, unchanging in the flux of history. Defending itself against the Enlightenment and a modernity hostile to religion, the ecclesiastical magisterium insisted even more on the unchanging nature of its teaching. The popes now thought of themselves as infallible. Catholics were told that in matters of faith and morals the magisterium taught an unchanging truth.

We saw in chapter 2 that Catholics living in modern society had religious experiences that changed their self-understanding and made them interpret the Gospel in an innovative way. The new faith experiences, supported by exegetes and theologians, persuaded the Second Vatican Council to change the Church's official teaching on several issues of faith and morals. Here are four examples: (1) The Council affirmed religious liberty that had been condemned by the papacy throughout the nineteenth and early twentieth century. (2) The Council praised and supported the ecumenical movement, condemned in 1928 in Pius XI's encyclical *Mortalium Animos*. (3) The Council recognized God's unbroken covenant with the Jewish people and expressed its respect for the world religions, no longer assigning them to the darkness of hell as the Church had done in the Good Friday Liturgy. (4) The Council acknowledged that the mystery of God's grace, revealed in Jesus Christ, is operative in the whole of human history, thus replacing the older teaching *extra ecclesiam nulla salus* (no salvation outside the Church).

These changes have produced theological headaches for the ecclesiastical magisterium. Official voices at the Vatican occasionally still speak as if the Church's official teaching never changes. Yet this discourse has lost credibility. The experience of the Council has had an effect on the perception of the magisterium by ordinary church-going Catholics. They recognize that, seeking fidelity to the Gospel in various historical situations, the magisterium relies on dialogue with the religious experience and the thought of the faithful. In the regime of Christendom, the popes condemned the principle of religious liberty because it undermined the stable unity of society. Yet in modern pluralistic society, the magisterium has been willing to listen – at first reluctantly, yet willingly at the Council – to the experience of the Catholic people and the ideas of their theologians. The magisterium now proclaims religious liberty as a Gospel imperative. It follows that the Church's magisterium, aided by the Holy Spirit, is always in process. That is why Catholics who today are unconvinced by a particular teaching of the magisterium feel free to follow their own profound convictions, formed by reflection on the Gospel in dialogue with their community. For instance, in Canada and Quebec, vast numbers of Catholics find the Anglican position on women and sexual ethics more convincing than present-day Catholic teaching. Dumont repeatedly refers to the contemporary situation as "a crisis of orthodoxy."[1] Through his theological and sociological reflections, he wants to make a contribution to resolving the present impasse.

To understand Dumont's thoughts on the relation between theology and the magisterium, we have to return to his teaching on faith. Christian faith, we recall, is a religious experience. Addressed by the divine message, Christians have faith, meaning they believe, repent, and reorient their lives. This faith is the work of the Spirit in their minds and hearts. Believers are impelled to express this experience and practice their faith in community. Faith is singular and at the same time constitutes a fellowship.

Dumont argues, as we have seen, that experience calls for expression, but that the expression never communicates the fullness of the experience. He spoke of the inevitable "distance" between the experience and its expression. The faith experience is thus richer than any articulation of it. Dumont interprets this "distance" as the source of creative tension: believers attentive to their social context are impelled to find ever-new ways of expressing their experience. At the same time, to protect the unity of the believing community, church authorities have formulated certain rules of faith or doctrines. The creeds they compose express the common redemptive story believed by the community of the baptized.

From the very beginning, Dumont notes, Christians were concerned with the cognitive content of their faith and reflected on it theologically. The apostles, especially St Paul and

St John, not only proclaimed the Good News; they also explored its meaning in rational terms and produced theological reflections. Theologians were active in the early Church. Among the various pastoral ministries, St Paul mentions specifically *doctores* (1 Cor 12:28; Eph 4:11), the thinkers and teachers in the Christian community.

Dumont notes that the relationship between the *doctores* and the ecclesiastical authorities has changed over the centuries. In the patristic age, theologians tended to be bishops and priests, members of the ecclesiastical hierarchy. In the Middle Ages, theologians located at the universities exercised great authority in the Church. St Thomas recognized the *cathedra magistralis* of theologians, distinct from the *cathedra pontificalis* of the pope and the *cathedra pastoralis* of the bishops. The medieval Church was open to theological pluralism and with few exceptions respected the public debate of doctrinal issues. Yet after the Reformation, hierarchy and theologians together defended the Catholic doctrines against the challenge of the Reformers. The competition among the divided Churches now persuaded the popes to demand greater theological uniformity in their Church. The magisterium we have at present, our author argues, is of more recent origin, beginning in the eighteenth century when the Church had to defend itself against the secular Enlightenment. In the nineteenth century, the popes became active as authoritative theological teachers: they multiplied the rules of faith, published encyclicals on doctrinal issues, limited the freedom of theologians, condemned theologians influenced by modern thought, and instituted an official theology and, in 1989, even an official philosophy.[2] The catechisms listing the teachings of the Catholic Church became ever bigger.

The papacy saw itself as the guardian of the deposit of faith conceived as a series of propositions, a pastoral policy that reduced divine revelation to its conceptual contents. Even theologians no longer insisted that divine revelation was much richer than its doctrinal expression. The few alternative voices in the nineteenth century, such as John Henry Newman and Karl Adam Möhler, were not heard. Dumont repeatedly mentions Cardinal Newman's observation that the Church Fathers regretted that certain false teachings obliged them to produced doctrinal definitions that tended to reduce the divine mystery to a series of concepts.

THE MULTIPLICATION OF DOCTRINES

Dumont argues that this multiplication of doctrines has deleterious consequences. Divine revelation here risks of being identified with a body of knowledge – a set of truths to be believed and commandments to be observed. There are indeed a few texts in the *Summa Theologica* of St Thomas that refer to divine revelation as a series of articles to be believed, yet the *Summa* as a whole refers to divine revelation as a mystery, as God's gracious self-communication to humanity. In the *Summa* both *fides qua* (the ground of faith) and *fides quae* (the object of faith) are ultimately God's gratuitous self-revelation (II-II, 1, 1). Yet under the influence of neo-scholasticism, the First Vatican Council (1870) spoke of divine revelation principally as a set of doctrines, a position that was widely followed by theologians. The return to the sources of faith in the twentieth century produced an important change of emphasis. Following these theologians, the Second Vatican Council recognized that divine revelation is God's self-revelation in Israel and finally in Jesus Christ:

His plan of revelation is realized by *deeds* and *words* having an inner unity: the *deeds* wrought by God in the history of salvation manifest and confirm the teaching and realities signified by the *words*, while the *words* proclaim the *deeds* and clarify the mystery contained in them. By this revelation then, the deepest truth about God and the

salvation of humankind is made clear to us in Jesus Christ
who is the Mediator and at the same time the fullness of
all revelation.[3]

Divine revelation took place in events and words: it is recorded in stories of salvation that have a doctrinal content,
but are not exhausted by it. Revelation is always richer than
any expression of it. Since Dumont puts great emphasis on
the inexhaustible character of God's revelation, he believes –
as we shall see – that in Scripture and Tradition God continues to address the believing community.

Dumont offers three reasons why the multiplication of doctrines by the magisterium has had deleterious effects on the
life of the Church. The ecclesiastical authorities have tried to
sustain and renew the faith of the Catholic people by enlarg-
ing the catechism and making its propositions more precise.
Our author thinks that this pastoral policy has been partially
responsible for the secularization of modern society and the
sudden loss of faith in Quebec.

We saw that Dumont looked upon the faith experience as
the work of the Spirit in people's lives. The magisterium and,
in line with it, the priests play an important role in the Church
as witnesses, guides, supervisors, and legislators, but they do
not produce the faith. Faith in Jesus is a gift of God. Priests,
bishops, and popes are ministers: they are meant to help the
faithful to enter more fully into the revealed truth and become
more effective public witnesses of their faith. Multiplying the
rules of faith has a problematic effect because it supposes that
Catholics remain believers by an act of obedience to the magisterium, rather than by their faith experience and their obedience to the Spirit. To believe by an act of obedience assures
doctrinal orthodoxy, but it does not generate life – it does not
provide inner strength nor release creativity. Instead of en-
couraging people to trust and pursue their own experience of
faith, the multiplication of doctrines, intended to produce
doctrinal conformity, promoted a religion of duty, passive

acceptance, and submission to authority. The long list of rules which the Quebec clergy imposed upon the people, Dumont argues, fostered belief by conformity, not a faith generated by personal experience. Once the clergy lost its power in the wake of the Quiet Revolution, Quebecers were no longer obliged to be obedient, and vast numbers of them declared themselves non-believers.

A second deleterious effect of the Church's identification of faith with obedience to a set of doctrines was that it persuaded Catholics to think that the many doctrines constituted a single system of divine truth, so that failing to believe in any one doctrine brought with it the collapse of the Catholic faith altogether. Faith based on obedience implies that all doctrines have an equivalent importance – the Incarnation as important as the Immaculate Conception, and the Resurrection as important as Mary's Assumption into Heaven. To move beyond this idea, the Second Vatican Council proposed that "Catholics should remember that in Catholic doctrine there exists 'a hierarchy' of truths, since they vary in their relation to the fundamental Christian faith."[4] Yet this is not the impression created by the old catechisms whose propositions were to be learnt by heart, nor by the new massive Catholic Catechism published by the Vatican in 1993. The endless list of doctrines makes Catholics forget that the Good News proclaimed to them intends to kindle their faith, make them see the world in a new light, and empower them to reorient their lives. Believing in one doctrine after another does not communicate spiritual rebirth.

Dumont raises a third point, rarely formulated in Catholic theology, to which he attaches great importance. When divine revelation is thought to be a series of truths, then to doubt any of them is regarded as a sin. According to the Church's traditional teaching, doubting is sinful.[5] Our author looks upon faith and doubt rather differently. In his philosophical work, he has introduced the distinction between truth and relevance. Truth addresses the mind: it may be abstract or make a concrete affirmation. Relevance is a special kind of truth, a truth that allows people to transcend an unsettling predicament or to resolve a conflict that preoccupies them. Truths that are unrelated to people's existential or historical problems have no power to transform their lives. In religion, Dumont holds, truth is not enough; what counts is relevance.

The Gospel is transformative truth; it addresses the plight in which the listeners find themselves and offers them insight, rescue, and freedom. The Gospel, Dumont insists, is ever relevant. As Christians move from one historical situation to another or from one culture to another, the message that sustained them in the past no longer addresses the urgent questions which they ask in the present. They must now have the courage to doubt and admit to themselves that the message they have inherited is no longer relevant. If they are unwilling to doubt, Dumont argues, they will cling to the old teaching that makes no sense to them and be unable to hear God's Word anew with a message relevant to their present condition. Troubled by doubts, some Catholics begin to think of themselves as unbelievers, instead of waiting in the dark, hoping to be addressed anew by God's Word in a manner relevant to their situation.

Dumont's reflections on doubt recall what he wrote about the passage from first to second culture, a process characterized as rupture and fidelity. His Catholic faith was challenged when he moved into the culture of the educated, yet with the help of the new theological thought in France he was able to discover the relevance of the Gospel to his present situation and to remain faithful to the Catholic heritage he received as a child. According to Dumont's dynamic anthropology, obstacles precede human creativity. Doubt remains for our author a dimension of people's living faith. We recall that for him 'reason in the basement' continues to ask challenging questions, doubt the inherited wisdom, and search for new answers – an intellectual activity that makes humans creative and opens the mind of believers to the ever richer meaning of the Gospel.

In his historical novel *Maître Eckhart*, the Quebec author Jean Bédard makes Eckhart, the German mystic, say to his assistant, "You must not confess your doubts, Conrad; doubting is no sin. It is actually a courageous expression of conscience."[6]

While Dumont is critical of the pastoral policies adopted by the magisterium, he recognizes as a sociologist that any society, including the Church, is in need of a government and an authoritative voice to articulate its values, policies, purpose, and orientation. The Church, he argues, needs a well-functioning magisterium. Before we turn to what he means by this, we must clarify several of his theological ideas.

REVELATION IN BIBLICAL FIGURES

For Dumont, as we have seen, faith is the experience of being addressed by the Gospel, of believing, repenting, and reorienting one's life. The believing community continues to be spoken to by God. As Christians move into a different historical situation, they discover that the Gospel utters a message relevant to their new context, a message they had not heard before. To shed light on the abiding relevance of the Gospel, Dumont sets forth that the Scriptures contain a never-ending number of *figures*, the meaning of which is inexhaustible. By *figures* Dumont means events or personalities described in the Bible that can be read as suggestive metaphors. I shall translate Dumont's term "la figure" by the English word "trope," which the Oxford English Dictionary defines as "a figurative or metaphorical use of a word or expression." The story of creation, the exodus from Egypt, the exile in Babylon, the birth of Jesus, his passion and crucifixion: these are all tropes rich in meaning. Persons such as Abraham, Moses, Jeremiah, and Jesus: they too are tropes that continue to express truth relevant to new situations.

Let me illustrate the multiple meanings of *les figures* or
tropes by a single example. The creation story, a foundational
biblical trope, is likely to be heard by a peasant or farmer as
God's blessing on the land and God's affirmation of his work
tilling the ground and producing food for his family and community. If the peasant is expelled from the land and works in
a factory at exploitative wages, the creation story loses its
relevance; yet as he listens to it again, he hears what it says
about the sin into which the world has fallen and recognizes
that the inhuman conditions imposed on him, as part of that
sin, stand under God's judgment. New labourers employed in
the factory are Muslim and Hindu immigrants who make the
worker feel uncomfortable, sharing as he does the popular
prejudice against them. If he now listens in faith to the creation story, he will hear that all human beings are children of
a single couple, Adam and Eve, and that the foreign labourers
are his brothers, a message that makes him repent of his prejudice and reorient his life. When some of his friends speak to
him of the ecological crisis, he is troubled by the sentence of
the creation story that calls upon humans "to subdue the
earth and be masters of all living creatures that move on
earth" (Gen 1:28). He is delivered from his doubts by his parish priest, who tells him that this passage was meant to encourage farmers to grow food for their community and tame
animals to become their helpers. The passage was not addressed to today's technological society.

What would happen if the worker, influenced by his contemporary culture, became troubled by the inequality between men and women in church and society? Listening again
to the creation story, he would be slightly consoled by the
sentence, "male and female created he them" (Gen 1:27). Yet
his anguish would not leave him. He would therefore decide
to look for other tropes in the Bible, for instance Jesus as divine reconciler, sent into the world to overcome the divisions
among humans created by inequality – between Jews and
other nations, between masters and slaves, and between men

and women (Gal 3:28). "God's Word continues to address us," the worker might say to his friends; "whenever I am confused in the darkness, I hear a new message." That the Word of God continues to address the believer and the believing community is a fundamental principle of Dumont's theology. To show that the divine summons does not simply produce religious fervour, but communicates concrete messages relevant for the believer, I wish to mention another biblical trope, this time following Dumont's own interpretation. In several pages of his book *Une foi partagée*, he offers a long description of the "figure" of Jesus presented in the four Gospels, that continues to address the believing community. I have summarized this description in *Truth and Relevance*:

> Dumont pays special attention to the historical Jesus announced in the synoptic gospels. Here Jesus is the prophet speaking with authority and announcing God's coming reign; at the same time, he is a man similar to us, troubled, exposed to temptations, capable of changing his mind, sometimes sad and sometimes joyful, in need of prayer and in search of friends. Jesus does not present himself as God incarnate; he is reticent about his identity; he seems to discover only gradually what his mission is. Dumont sees Jesus as an enigmatic personality not at home in any of the religious circles or parties of his day. He is powerful and vulnerable, sovereign and humble, a follower of the Law and independent of it, conservative (protecting the local culture against Rome's imperial invasion) and radical (critical of the official interpretation of his religion). Psychology is unable to solve the riddle of his personality: he appears unique, inimitable, mysterious.
>
> This Jesus, Dumont continues, is utterly attractive, and at the same time deeply disturbing. He raises questions about our lives, demands that we change our ways, and calls us to love God and our neighbour. Jesus will not

leave us alone; he continues to challenge our selfishness
and encourages our efforts to follow his lead. Our conversation with him is without end. Jesus utters different messages at different occasions, depending on the challenges
we encounter in our concrete situations. In his earthly life,
he challenged the religious authorities and the imperial
rule, even though his prophetic witness would cost him his
life. Dumont is not surprised that the message of Jesus
heard by Christians, including biblical scholars, is related
to the profound questions that trouble them. He fully understands that oppressed people hear in the Gospel the
promise of liberation. Jesus sheds light on the lives of people whatever their situation. His figure transforms their
existence; his message is ever relevant.[7]

Listening to the figure of Jesus provides more wisdom and
more motivation to act than reflecting on the doctrinal definition of Jesus, as true man and true God, the Word incarnate
or the second Person of the Holy Trinity. Dumont recognizes
the need to clarify the concepts implicit in divine revelation,
and he embraces the doctrines defined by the early ecumenical
councils, yet he demonstrates that divine revelation is far
richer in meaning and redemptive power than its reduction to
dogma. As mentioned several times before, it is faith, religious
experience – to be spoken to, believe, repent, and reorient
one's practice – that creates the Church and renews it. He
thinks that the Church's nervous preoccupation with orthodoxy lacks pastoral wisdom. It is possible to embrace orthodox teaching without being inwardly sustained and made
alive. Strict obedience is able to create unanimity in the
Christian community, yet it does not provide access to the
sources of faith nor communicate new life.

   Dumont's books and articles on religion reveal that he himself accepts the Church's orthodox creed. Yet since he did not
regard orthodoxy as the major pastoral concern, he wondered
whether the division of the Christian Church at the time

of the Reformation had really been necessary, especially since the great majority of Christians, whether Catholic or Protestant, wanted the same thing, namely to practice faith and hope and love God and their neighbour. All Christians believed that Jesus Christ was present at the celebration of Holy Communion. What is not clear is why the ecclesiastical authorities made the mode of Christ's presence the centre of a deeply dividing doctrinal debate. While doctrine plays a necessary part in the Church, our author asked himself whether its place in the Church's proclamation of the Good News has been correctly understood.

LA RÉFÉRENCE: IDENTIFICATION WITH THE CATHOLIC TRADITION

To understand how Dumont sees the relation of theologians to the magisterium, we still have to look at his innovative ecclesiological reflections.[8] Being part of a collectivity, our author argues, occurs in a variety of ways that can be usefully divided into three types. First, we are part of a community by *belonging* if we know its members personally, engage in conversation with them, and decide together how the community should live and act. Membership by belonging occurs in villages, small parishes, base communities, cooperatives, and many other small organizations. Because here people decide together how to define themselves and how to engage in action, they make few fixed rules.

Second, we are part of a collectivity by *integration* if our membership assigns us a place in the institution, defines our rights and duties, and obliges us to obey the rules made by the governing authorities. In this manner we belong to a university, a government ministry, an industrial or commercial corporation, and many other large institutions. To function well, institutions of this kind need a directorship that defines the rules that regulate the activity of the members. It is possible to interpret the Church as an institution in which believers

become members by integration. Dumont argues that in order
to reform the clergy, control the members, and centralize the
ruling authority, the Catholic Church has greatly emphasized
its organizational character. It has produced extensive legislation, insisted on doctrinal conformity, and made itself into a
giant bureaucracy, in which believers-become-members are
assigned their place and their duties.

   Dumont proposes a third way of being part of a collectivity,
such as being a member of a nation or belonging to a country.
This is not "belonging" because the members remain largely
unknown to us, nor is this "integration" since nations or
countries are not organizations. We belong to a nation by
"référence," a word used by Dumont that I shall freely translate as "symbolic identification." To be part of a collectivity
by "référence" means sharing its memory and having hope
for its future. The shared memory may be the nation's foundation, important events in its history, its cultural achievements, and the brilliant personalities that have affected its
self-understanding in the past and the present. While aware
of our nation's unjust practices, we remember its cultural and
spiritual resources for doing good and practicing justice, thus
retaining hope for a better future. Even if people disapprove
of the present government and disagree with its social philosophy, they continue to identify with their nation and are
ready to serve it. When Paul Tillich opposed the Nazi regime
in 1933 and fled the country, he was accused by a former
friend, the Protestant theologian Emanuel Hirsch, of betray-
ing his fatherland. Tillich replied that those who truly love
their country want it to be just.

   Dumont argues that Catholics belong to the Church by "référence," by symbolic identification, sharing a common memory and a common hope. Catholics remember the events of
God's revelation, first in the Old Testament and later in the
redemptive work of Christ; they remember the early Christian
community, the practice of baptism, the Eucharistic liturgy,
and many other important events in the Church's history,

including the saints that have impressed them and the cathedrals, sculptures, and paintings they have admired. The great events of the past assume symbolic meaning for them: their shared past defines who they are as a believing community. Despite the bad memories – the Church's hostility to outsiders, its anti-Jewish rhetoric, its past approval of torture and inquisition, and its alliances with the powerful, including dictators – Catholics believe that the resources for compassion and social justice in the Church's tradition allow them to have hope for a better future. If the ecclesiastical government disappoints them, and even if they disagree with some of its pastoral policies, they nonetheless belong to the Church by *référence*, by symbolic identification. That is why critical Catholics can say that they are deeply rooted in the Catholic tradition.

THE THEOLOGIAN SERVES THE MAGISTERIUM

We now return to the question of this chapter on the relationship of the theologian to the magisterium. Dumont, as we have seen, regards theologians as mediators. They mediate the insights and aspirations of the believing community to the various levels of the magisterium. This took place in a dramatic way during the Second Vatican Council when theologians were invited to address the various bishops' conferences gathered at Rome and appointed as *periti* or experts on the conciliar commissions to prepare the draft documents for the Council.

Theologians also mediate the teaching of the magisterium to the believing community. They explain to the people the biblical foundation and the theological meaning of the Church's official teaching and its pastoral policies. This mediation, Dumont notes, is done in a variety of ways. Some theologians think it is their duty to communicate the official teaching and defend it with theological arguments. According to Pius XII's encyclical *Humani Generis* (1950), the highest task of the theologian is to demonstrate that the teaching of the magisterium is in perfect conformity with the sources of faith in Scripture and Tradition.[9] Dumont sees this differently. He offers a sociological argument to show that in mediating the Church's official teaching to the believing community, theologians may not abandon their critical function.

Every society, Dumont argues, produces an official story and a set of ideas that justify its existence and legitimize its governing authority. Our author calls these an "ideology," an expression that has a positive meaning for him. Societies are in need of an ideology. At the same time, the ideology that legitimizes the existing society must remain open to the critical responses of its members. Without the critical reflection of the people, the ideology will assume a rigid character and become a fixed and unchanging theory that prevents society from reacting creatively to the changing circumstances of history. A critique of ideology is necessary for the well-being of society. According to our author, the Church as an organization produces an ideology to justify its governmental structure and at the same time needs a critique of its ideology to overcome its inflexibility and open itself to future developments. It follows that in mediating the Church's official teaching to the believing community, theologians also raise questions and point to unresolved issues. We have seen above that Dumont looks upon intellectuals, including theologians, as critical thinkers with a prophetic mission in the society to which they belong. Theologians are grateful to the magisterium for the guardianship it exercises in the believing community, yet they are also critical of the magisterium when its ideology prevents it from hearing God's Word addressed to the believing community in the present.

As a baptized believer and theologian, Dumont raises critical questions regarding the style of teaching adopted by the magisterium in modern times. As I mentioned above, he fears that the multiplication of doctrinal and pastoral rules persuades Catholics that divine revelation consists of truths to be believed and commandments to be obeyed. Over the last centuries, our author argues, the Catholic Church has increasingly understood itself as a giant organization and considered Catholic believers to be members by "integration," occupying an assigned place and exercising a defined role in the Church, controlled by a vast set of regulations. The multiplication of rules makes Catholics believers by obedience: this renders them orthodox, yet does not spark religious experience nor rekindle the life of faith. A major reason for the wave of unbelief that has passed through Quebec society, Dumont argues, is that the people were largely believers by obedience, not sustained in their faith by religious experience.

Divine revelation, as we have seen, takes place in events accompanied by words explaining their meaning. God's Word is made known in the witnesses and stories of Scripture that provide, beyond their cognitive content, meaning and inspiration that address the anguish, the ideals, and the questions people have in the changing circumstances of their lives. The principal task of the ecclesial magisterium, our author argues, is to protect and strengthen *la référence*, the symbolic identification of Catholics with the events of salvation and the witnesses across the ages. The testimonies of the magisterium that give concrete expression of love, compassion, justice, and fidelity to truth confirm the Catholic identity of believers, renew their commitment to the Church, and make them grateful to the Holy Spirit who accompanies the believing community in its history. It is counter-productive for the magisterium, our author thinks, to see itself as a court of justice that settles issues remote from the biblical message that are seriously debated in the believing community. The will to impose unanimity on the Church disguises *la référence*: it weakens the life-giving identification of Catholics with the Church's redemptive witness across the ages.

Our author thinks that the magisterium should recognize a certain theological pluralism in the Church. Since Catholics belong to a variety of cultures, they interpret the Gospel and its exigencies in dialogue with their own culture and in doing so produce a rich diversity in the unity of *la référence*, the

common commitment to the events of salvation announced in
Scripture and Tradition. Dumont's proposal agrees with the
famous principle of the ancient Church, "In essentials unity,
in non-essentials liberty, in all cases charity."

I wish to support Dumont's bold proposal with reference to
a contemporary event. In 2008 the Roman Congregation of
the Doctrine of the Faith decided to investigate the Leadership
Conference of Women Religious (LCWR), the great organization representing 57,000 women religious in the USA. These
women were suspected of disagreeing with the Church's official teaching on women and sexuality. Since the reaction of the
LCWR was deemed unsatisfactory, the Roman Congregation
launched a second investigation in 2012. Vast number of
Catholics were appalled by this undertaking, and publicly expressed their support for the sisters. These women serve the
poor and the weak in their society; they work in hospitals,
parishes, schools, orphanages, retirement homes, and many
other places where people need help. They speak out in favour of social justice, human rights, international peace, and
political policies in support of women and the marginalized
groups in society. For ordinary Catholics these women confirm *la référence*: they strengthen the identification of believers with the Catholic tradition. They give witness to the love,
justice, compassion, and fidelity to truth summoned forth by
the Christian Gospel. The will of the magisterium to impose
unanimity on these women in regard to issues that are seriously debated in the believing community runs counter to *la
référence*. Instead of confirming the identification of Catholics
with the events of salvation and the witnesses throughout the
ages, it makes them uncomfortable with the Catholicism they
have inherited.

AFFIRMING *LA RÉFÉRENCE*

According to Dumont, as we saw above, the primary task of
the magisterium is to guard and reinforce *la référence*, the

symbolic identification of the believing community with the events and the history of salvation. In their role as mediators, theologians also seek to strengthen *la référence*. What this entails is explored by Dumont in chapter 5 of *L'institution de la théologie*. The faithful themselves, our author insists, reaffirm the symbolic identification with the Catholic tradition by the witness they give of their faith. Since the essential truths of the Catholic faith are clearly proclaimed in the Catholic liturgy, especially in the Creed and the Gloria, the task of the magisterium is to confirm these truths by giving a credible witness to them in its pastoral policies. Already Vatican Council I in 1871 called the Church "the perpetual motive of credibility":[10] its concrete historical existence is here seen as a universally valid argument that the Gospel is a credible message. Even as a visible organization, the Church should give witness of its faith in Jesus Christ. The relationship within it between the rulers and the ruled should be a model of mutual respect, justice, wide consultation, and freedom, witnessing its divine origin. In the statement "Justice in the World" published by the World Synod of Bishops in 1971, we read,

> While the Church is bound to give witness to justice, it recognizes that everyone who ventures to speak to people about justice, must first be just in their eyes. Hence we must undertake an examination of the models of acting and of possession and life style found within the Church itself.[11]

To give a persuasive witness to the Gospel, the statement continues, the Church must recognize the human rights of its members, their suitable freedom of thought and expression, their right to be heard in a spirit of dialogue, and the capacity of believers to have a share in the decisions made by the authorities.

A similar point is made in the pastoral letter "Economic Justice for All" of the American Catholic bishops in 1986.

The Church, they say, that advocates social justice and solidarity with the powerless in society must make a critical review of its own pastoral practice: it has to embody in its own institutional existence the virtues it urges upon society. The American bishops then promise that "as we have proposed a new experiment in collaboration and participation in decision making by all those affected at all levels of US society, so we also commit the Church to become a model of collaboration and participation."[12] This was, alas, an empty promise. Since the 1980s, the Church has increasingly become a symbol of authoritarianism, non-participation, and the absence of internal dialogue.

The Church is not a democracy, nor is it a monarchy or an oligarchy. The Church of Jesus Christ is not fashioned in the image of a secular society. The Church is a community of believers, endowed with many gifts, including an appointed authority that teaches and continues to learn, listening to the Spirit speaking in the community. Dumont writes,

> If this is so, the magisterium may not be defined as the unique authority setting down the norms of faith or even its pastoral regulations. The magisterium has never simply been, nor is it today, an agency that produces texts. By their pastoral activity, the pope and the bishops are first of all the guardians of a heritage and a unity that transcends the texts.[13]

The important task of the ecclesiastical magisterium is to guard the life-giving divine truth received by the Church, in dialogue with the believing community and attentive to the insights and values of the culture it inhabits. The truth that the Church guards is richer and deeper than the defined doctrine. This truth addresses mind and heart, transforms the life of believers, and manifests itself in the Church's witness, its compassion, its love of God and neighbour, and its commitment to justice. The function of the magisterium is to strengthen the symbolic identification of the Catholic community with the events of salvation and the witnesses of faith throughout the ages. To confirm this life-giving identification, the magisterium is not primarily a complaint department that hunts after errors; its first task is to bless and encourage the ideas and practices of Catholics that make them witnesses of the Catholic tradition. Dumont wants the Church to be an authoritative teacher of the Gospel even through the style of its own organization, open to dialogue with the believing community and in solidarity with the poor and people in need. For Dumont the true character of the Church's magisterium became manifest at the Second Vatican Council: here bishops and the pope formulated their teaching after listening to the experience of the faithful, rereading Scripture and Tradition, paying attention to theologians, and learning from the insights of modern culture. Nor was the magisterium at the Council unwilling to change its mind on important ethical issues, such as human rights and respect for religious pluralism. Guided by the Holy Spirit, the magisterium is ever in process.

According to Dumont, the magisterium should respect theological pluralism in the Church, leave open doctrinal issues that are seriously debated in the believing community, and recognize distinctive forms of Catholicism in response to diverse national or regional cultures.

Many readers will find Dumont's theology of the magisterium very bold. I was surprised to find similar ideas in the writings of Cardinal Franz König († 2004), Archbishop of Vienna from 1956 to 1985.

The primary concern of the Catholic Church, in whose name I speak, must always be to pass on the Gospel message with its partly adaptable and partly unalterable truth. I am thus faced with the question: how do I fulfill my task of conveying the Gospel in today's world? It is not an easy task and requires much more than it used to – honest cooperation between bishops, priests and laity. Here, too, it was the Second Vatican Council that repeatedly pointed to the necessity of such cooperation. As *Lumen gentium* #33 says "Now, the laity are called in a special way to make the Church present and fruitful in places and circumstances where only through them can it become the salt of the earth." This, too, is the reason why Church leaders should not be afraid of too great diversity. Over the years their fears in this respect have led to an excessive and defensive centralism and bureaucracy. Ever since the Second Vatican Council, it has become increasingly clear that the Catholic Church faces a problem of a particular kind in the future. The Catholic faithful in the parishes and dioceses lose heart when they receive no reassurance and comfort from the central Church leadership, when – with the exception of documents and encyclicals written by the Pope himself ... warnings of errors and heresies predominate in the countless documents that pour out of Rome. The Catholic faithful expect signs of encouragement and a mutual flow of information as a sign of unity and of diversity.[14]

4

The Theologian and Tradition

It is possible to understand tradition as the ideas, values, and practices that persons or groups inherited from the past and that are part of their present culture. Here fidelity to the past creates a conservative social outlook, cultural conformity, resistance to new ideas, and unwillingness to recognize the dark side of one's own history. This is not what Dumont understands by tradition! Still, the inherited memory and customs have their own usefulness: they enable us to do our daily work, meet the people that surround us, and behave appropriately in society.

THE RECOVERY OF TRADITION

To illustrate what he understands by tradition, Dumont offers the following reflection. He notes that the inherited memory does not help us to respond when something unexpected happens to us: the loss of employment, a grave accident, or the death of a loved one. Here we have to respond creatively. We have to draw strength from our identity as a person, ask ourselves how rooted we are in a community, and reflect on our past, on who we were and who we have become. While we recognize our vulnerability and finitude, we have to embrace our life courageously as a wager. Without a measure of hope, no door will be open to the future. In wrestling with this personal issue, we have to rethink our past, look upon it in a new light, and redefine our personal identity. In this process, we are not alone: we seek support from others and draw upon resources we have previously disregarded. In response to a serious obstacle, we acquire a new relation to history, discover a tradition that sustains us, and experience a measure of hopefulness.

I read this paragraph in *L'institution de la théologie*[1] with some emotion since it illumines and clarifies my own experience when in 1939, at the age of fifteen, I became a refugee from Germany.

For Dumont, tradition results from the rereading of history in the light of the moral exigencies of the present. Our author often refers to this as "historical consciousness." Tradition provides memory and hope for a creative entry into the future.

Let me illustrate this abstract analysis by reflecting in an imaginative way on the experience of Dumont's father that I mentioned in chapter 1. When this hard-working labourer sees the harness forced upon the neck of the horses, he has a sudden insight into the enslavement inflicted upon him and his fellow workers. He now recognizes that being a human person, he is not meant to be a slave. He now finds fault with the heartless capitalist economy, as well as with the conformist culture he has inherited. He now rethinks his childhood and the teaching he received in his parish. If he talks about his experience with his fellow workers, he will discover with them that they are part of a worldwide movement: the struggle of labour for social justice. He now can say, I belong to a tradition and that is why I have hope. His experience has led to a new relationship to history.

Dumont's reflections on experience and tradition reaffirm his anthropological thesis, mentioned in chapter 1, that all human beings have faith. Being finite and ending in death, human life remains forever unfulfilled, yet we keep on striving for greater fulfillment, and even when confronted with many obstacles, we do not give up. We continue the struggle because we are moved by a faith and thus are not devoid of hope. According to Dumont's anthropology, believing (*le croire*) sustains our will to live and orients our lives. Knowing and acting follow.

As we saw in chapter 1, Dumont relates the desire to transcend finitude to the presence of a nameless Transcendence in our lives:

> If you do not let go and are ready to put your trust in memory and hope, the endeavour will go on without limit, all the while trying to give it meaning. To arrive at this, the endeavour has to relate itself to a transcendence. This relation is implicit in the consciousness of our finitude. We only become aware of this when we contrast our limits with a representation of an Infinite.[2]

Rereading the past and discovering that one is sustained by a great tradition is also experienced by collectivities. Their experience involves faith and hope. Let me illustrate this with a brief reflection on the students' strike of 2012 in Quebec. The students recognized that by raising the fees for university education, the government was increasing social inequality, limiting education to young people of well-to-do families and forcing all others to take on loans that would burden them for years to come. They realized that the government wants universities to be run increasingly like commercial institutions, with students as clients buying their education and professors as employees subject to regulations made by the administration. The students' strike was supported by educators and other thoughtful Quebecers opposed to the entry of the market mentality into the university. While the government thought that the quarrel was simply about money, the students and the educators saw it as a debate over the philosophy of education. The students discovered that during the Quiet Revolution, the Parent Commission had recommended free public education, eventually including even university studies.[3] They also remembered that massive demonstrations have occasionally raised public awareness and affected political change. Transcending the widespread individualism of contemporary culture, they succeeded in organizing a protest movement that embraced tens of thousands of students over several months, with occasional demonstrations supported by 200,000 Quebecers. Using Dumont's vocabulary, the students may well have said to one another, "we have rethought our relation to history"; "we now belong to a tradition"; and "we have inherited a measure of hope."

SCRIPTURE AND TRADITION

Human experience in response to an obstacle prompts the recovery of a tradition that provides memory and hope. Dumont argued that this also applies to the faith experience of Christians. It too responds creatively to obstacles by re-reading the past and discovering a tradition that provides memories and hope. Relying on their faith, Christians challenged by disturbing questions will turn to the Scriptures and the Church's experience throughout the ages in the hope of hearing God's Word addressed to them and finding guidance and strength. The saving messages they hear constitute Tradition with a capital T. Tradition in the theological sense refers to words, events, and persons remembered in the Bible and in Christian history that communicate meaning and salvation to believers in response to their present predicaments.

A characteristic of Dumont's entire philosophical work is the conviction that there is an affinity between human experience and Christian experience. We saw in chapter 1 that believing is the underlying orientation of all human beings and that Christian faith, while altogether particular, fits into this universal pattern. Dumont sees a similar affinity between human experience in the face of an obstacle becoming creative through memory and hope, and Christian experience in response to a challenge becoming creative in reliance on memory and hope found in Scripture and Christian history. For Dumont, there is a certain coherence between nature and grace. While Christian faith is a divine gift and not simply a human product, it does correspond to universally present human experience, which in its own way involves believing, memory, and hope.

In chapter 4, Dumont stresses again that the memory of the Church, the deposit of faith, may not be reduced to a list of doctrines to be believed and commandments to be obeyed. Arguing against the Protestant principle of *sola scriptura*, the Council of Trent insisted that the *depositum fidei* was present in Scripture and Tradition, a debate that assumed divine revelation was a set of truths. Dumont repeats that divine revelation has taken place in events and words. The Gospel is not only a summary of the sayings of Jesus, but includes his actions and symbolic gestures. Our author regards the Gospel as a living message. We recall his analysis of figures or tropes that continue to address the believing community. For Dumont, Christianity does not have a definable essence; it is rather a living historical movement created by the community of believers who reread the Scriptures and listen to the witnesses of faith throughout the ages. This is true of all world religions: they too are created by believing communities faithful to sacred texts, ritual gestures, and the memory of the witnesses.

To move beyond a purely conceptual idea of faith, Dumont attaches great importance to the witness of faith. Witnessing is a confession of faith, vouched by an action or by assuming a risk. The important personalities of the Bible were witnesses. They confirmed their faith by courageous deeds, resistance to power, fidelity under difficult circumstances, or even the sacrifice of their lives. Our author also honours the witnesses in the Church's history. They confirmed their faith by bold actions, and in doing so, interpreted the meaning of the Gospel for their age. Exegetes and theologians help the Church to interpret the Scriptures, but in Dumont's perspective, focusing as he does on Christian experience, the witnesses, be they prominent personalities or simple believers, are also reliable interpreters. They discover the relevance of the Gospel for the people of their own culture. These witnesses are part of Tradition with a capital T.

In his book *Une foi partagée*, Dumont has two chapters on witnesses which analyze how testifying to one's faith in public transforms the self-understanding of the believer and seriously challenges the observers, making them ask questions they previously avoided.[4] Among the witnesses, Dumont mentions personalities of the present age, some well-known like Emmanuel Mounier and Simone Weil, and others, men and women, known in Quebec for living a life of faith, hope, and charity. The witnesses from biblical times to the present day are part of Tradition. They belong to what Dumont has called *la référence*, which I have freely translated as symbolic representation. Catholics belong to the Church, our author argues, by a believing identification with the events and symbols of salvation and with the cloud of witnesses throughout history.

For our author, Scripture and Tradition are not two distinct sources of Christian faith. Divine revelation takes place in events accompanied by words that disclose their meaning. Believers respond to divine revelation by believing, repenting, and giving witness, thus constituting a tradition. Later, some members of the community are inspired to record the witnesses in writing, producing the Scriptures that the Church accepts as the fixed norm for all subsequent proclamation. Scripture and Tradition cohere: one cannot be accessed without the other. This reflection leads our author to two important questions in regard to the work of the theologian. First, in what sense are the Scriptures the abiding norm of Christian faith? And second, what does fidelity to Tradition mean?

THE BIBLE AS DEFINITIVE NORM

We are not surprised that Dumont's reflection on Scripture and Tradition does not begin with Christian faith as a calm conviction acquired in childhood. Throughout *L'institution de la théologie*, he looks upon Christian faith as an experience, a believing response to present confusions, ready to question inherited presuppositions. In traditional societies, Christian faith was often part of the first culture, yet since every culture is challenged by some of its adherents, it is liable to split open (*le dédoublement*) and give rise to a second culture. This passage from the first to the second culture has an unsettling impact on faith and produces doubts. Such a crisis of faith is overcome by new religious experiences of the believing community and by the work of theologians, returning to the sources of faith in Scripture and Christian history. Dumont writes,

> The memory of the Christian has not received the promise of quietly possessed certitude. Certitude, as its etymology suggests, implies fidelity. Doubt is alive in it as its indispensible depth. This memory resembles all other fidelities: its vitality lies even in its uncertainties, and that is why it is attentive not only to God but also to its finitude as a twofold sign of its authenticity.[5]

The task of the theologian is to listen to the new religious experience, reread the Scriptures, examine the tradition, and try to formulate the relevance of the Gospel for the present culture. For Dumont, following the common teaching, the Scriptures are the permanent norm of the Church's teaching. This does not mean that to be recognized as valid, a Christian faith experience must be confirmed by a biblical text. We recall that for Dumont the Scriptures constitute a living voice that addresses the believing community in its concrete historical condition. For him the biblical message cannot be equated with a series of texts. The Bible contains stories and personalities that constitute figures or tropes that are rich in meaning, capable of replying to present questions in an innovative way. To critique and validate a Christian experience, it is not necessary that it be confirmed by a particular biblical text; what is required is that the experience be tested by Scripture – that is to say, that biblical figures or tropes confirm that it corresponds to God's revealed Word.

Let me illustrate this with reference to the three recent Christian experiences mentioned in chapter 2: (1) the divine call to co-responsibility for the world; (2) God's redemptive presence in the whole of history; and (3) solidarity with dissident Christians and followers of the world religions.

The Divine Call for Historical Responsibility

That kings are responsible for the well-being of their societies is found in the Scriptures. By contrast, that society as a human construction can be dismantled and reconstructed by humans is a discovery of the modern age. At the end of the eighteenth century (after the French Revolution) and in the nineteenth century, the emerging modern insight challenged the Catholic Church which regarded the feudal-aristocratic order as part of God's providence and called upon the faithful to remain obedient to their prince. The magisterium repudiated human rights, religious liberty, and the principles of democracy. Yet in the twentieth century, living in modern society, Catholics came to believe that implicit in the Gospel were respect for human rights and the call for responsible participation in the making of society. These beliefs had to be tested by the Scriptures. While there are no biblical texts that vouch for them, theologians inquired whether these beliefs were in keeping with the Scriptures and corresponded to God's Word. This was done famously in John XXIII's encyclical *Pacem in Terris* (1963). The pope refers to the creation of men and women in the image of God and to Christ's desire to have all humans become his friends.[6] Relying on these two biblical figures, the pope concludes that human beings have a high dignity grounded in God's Word that calls for universal respect and offers a theological foundation for human rights, religious liberty, and other democratic values. Previous popes did not hear this message in the Scriptures. Yet living in a modern society and being impressed by the Universal Declaration of Human Rights of 1948, John XXIII reread the Bible and heard in it a new message. This illustrates what Dumont means by testing a new religious experience by the Scriptures.

God as Personal Presence in History

Do Blondel's and Dumont's experiences of God find support in the Scriptures? Are panentheism or redemptive immanence in keeping with God's Word? The Scriptures record that the perception of God changes as believers move from one culture to another. Hebrew religious texts spoke of God in cosmological images: God enthroned in the heavens, raised high above the earth. Even in the New Testament, the entry of Jesus into God's glory is still described as an ascension, an upward movement toward the sky. Yet the apostles could not use these cosmological images when proclaiming the Gospel in a Hellenist culture. The Greeks had an inkling that God was the hidden reality that sustains all beings and pervades the universe. Paul reminded the Athenians that their poets already said that in God "we live and move and have our being" (Acts 17:28). Adapting Greek philosophical images, John proclaimed that "God is Love, and whoever lives in love lives in God and God in him" (1 John 4:16). The transition from Hebrew to Hellenistic images is a biblical figure that addresses the Church of our own day, summoning it to find a discourse about God that would make the Gospel more credible in modern culture. Needed is a discourse about God that, instead of distracting people from their earthly concerns, makes them take with utmost seriousness their co-responsibility for their historical context. The panentheistic interpretation does this. It also gives new and rich meaning to the abstract nouns used in the Scriptures to refer to God: God as Love, Life, and Light.

Solidarity with the Entire Humanity

Ecumenism and the openness to religious pluralism, supported by contemporary Catholic experience, also need to be
tested by Scripture. This is not easy. The Church has read the
Scriptures by focusing on the passages that limit salvation to
believers in Jesus, obedient to the Church. "No salvation outside the Church" has been a traditional ecclesiastical principle. In the second part of the twentieth century, affected by
the pluralism of modern society, Catholics found it increasingly impossible to practice the traditional intolerance.
Listening to the biblical figure of Jesus as "*salvator mundi*"
and "lover of all human beings," they came to recognize that
their faith obliges them to embrace all human beings as their
neighbour, whatever their religion. Catholic theologians now
acknowledge the devastating historical consequences of the
inherited exclusivist teaching, such as contempt for outsiders,
persecution of dissidents, prejudice against Jews, wars of religion, and the blessing of colonialism. This traditional teaching, theologians now argue, did not pay adequate attention to
the full message of Jesus Christ. The commandment to love
God and one's neighbour, which sums up the entire ethics of
the Bible, demands the rethinking of the Church's relation
to outsiders.

In his book *A Secular Age*, Charles Taylor argues that the
intellectual starting point for the secularization of European
society was the philosophy of universal peace and justice developed by thinkers of the seventeenth and eighteenth centuries.[7] He mentions in particular Justus Lipsius († 1606) and
Hugo Grotius († 1645). They proposed a social philosophy
that protected the well-being of all human beings. Christian
charity, they argued, stops at the boundaries of the Church:
Christians do not love heretics, Jews, or pagans. Their worldly philosophy of universal solidarity, suggests Charles Taylor,
offered a dignified alternative of Christianity, initiating the
secularization of culture.

I wish to mention another witness to universal solidarity: an eighteenth-century philosopher who gave up on Christianity because the Churches were allied with the kings and rulers of the world. Critical of the universal truth claims made by certain French and English Enlightenment thinkers, Johann Gottfried Herder († 1803) defended the linguistic and cultural pluralism of the human race. He denounced the colonialism of the European powers because they humiliated and enslaved the peoples of other continents:

> What, finally, are we to say of the civilization and culture that the Spaniards, the Portuguese, the English and the Dutch have brought to the East and West Indies and among the Negroes of Africa? Are not these countries crying out for revenge now that they find themselves plunged for an indefinite period of time into mounting disaster? If there were such a thing as a European collective spirit ... it could not but feel ashamed of the crimes committed by us, having insulted mankind in a manner such as scarcely any other group of nations had done.[8]

The alliance of the Churches with the colonizing empires is not part of what Dumont calls Tradition with a capital T.

The work done by Catholic theologians in the second part of the twentieth century allowed the Second Vatican Council to change the Church's official teaching in regard to outsiders, be they dissidents, atheists, or followers of other religions. While defending its uniqueness and authenticity, the Catholic Church now respects the other Christian Churches, acknowledges the work of the Spirit in their midst, and joins them in the ecumenical movement for Christian unity. The Second Vatican Council also corrected the Church's traditional anti-Jewish rhetoric. Rereading the Pauline assurance that "God has never abandoned his own people" (Rom 11:2), the Council acknowledged God's abiding love of the first-chosen people and the ongoing validity of God's ancient covenant with them. Vatican II also honoured the world religions, acknowledging that an echo of God's Word resounds in them and that the Church shares many of their insights and values.

This doctrinal development broke with tradition. What has taken place, in Dumont's vocabulary, is *rupture* and *fidelity*. Rereading the Scriptures, the Church now pays attention to passages, previously overlooked, that present the biblical figure of "Jesus, lover of all humans." Significant is here the attitude of Jesus toward the Samaritans rejected as heretics by the Jewish religious authorities. He spoke to them as friends and made a Samaritan (Lk 10:29–37) the symbol of selfless love of neighbour. The Good Samaritan is in fact Jesus himself, whose love includes all human beings, insiders as well as outsiders, especially the weak and the wounded. Significant is also the biblical message that people relate themselves to the God of salvation by their way of life and their actions. "Whoever does the will of my Father in heaven is brother, sister and mother to me" (Mt 12:50). Practicing love, justice, and peace, people of whatever background join the family of Jesus. In his Sermon on the Mount, he proclaimed the beatitudes, virtues that could be practiced in any religion. In the famous parable in Matthew 25, Jesus tells people who have come to the aid of the weak, the poor, and the excluded – "the least of the brethren" – that they are doing this to him, the Christ, even if they have never heard of him (Mt 25:40). In the Incarnation, God has embraced the whole of humanity, beginning with the marginal and deserted. There are thus good reasons to claim that the Church's new openness to the world and its new respect for religious pluralism are in keeping with the Scriptures.

The Scriptures are the abiding norm of Christian faith: all Christian religious experience must be tested and approved by them. Dumont has great confidence in the interpretation of Scripture in the patristic age and the conceptual clarification of biblical revelation by the early Ecumenical Councils.

He refers to these as "second Scripture." Despite his tren-
chant critique of the reduction of God's Word to a series of
revealed truths, he does not overlook the cognitive content
of divine revelation. He argues that the Church Fathers who
defined the central Christian doctrines preserved a sense
of the divine mystery and the unknowability of God, and
had no intention of equating Christian faith with a system
of ideas. As I mentioned above, Dumont cites a remark of
Cardinal Newman that the bishops of antiquity regretted
that the errors of dissident Christians obliged them to make
doctrinal definitions.

Dogma easily makes people believe that divine revelation is
a set of ideas. Despite his many warnings, our author – as we
shall see in chapter 5 – appreciates and explores the conceptual truths of Christian faith and recognizes the task of dog-
matic theology.

FIDELITY TO TRADITION

The theologian must also be faithful to Tradition. He or she
has to examine critically whether the religious experience of
the believing community is in keeping with the witnesses of
faith throughout the ages. The theologian's turn to the past is
not the equivalent of studying the Church's history. We saw
in the preceding paragraphs that the Church's contempt for
outsiders (dissidents, Jews, and pagans), part of its history
over centuries, is no longer regarded as normative. The theologian rereads the history of the believing community in the
light of the urgent questions raised by Christians of the present. Our author calls this the creation of "historical consciousness." The theologian focuses on the historical witnesses
that support, purify, and clarify the faith experience of the
believing community to which he or she belongs. These witnesses our author designates as Tradition with a capital T. To
the Church's Tradition belong love of neighbour, compassion
for the weak, and help extended to the poor, practiced by

Christians throughout the centuries. The long history of the Catholic contempt for outsiders is not part of the Tradition.

As the Church moves from one culture to another, it must respond in a creative way to the truth, the values, and the errors of its new environment, a theological task of the believing community that calls for the rereading of its history and the rethinking of its inherited teaching. To illustrate the shock experienced by the Catholic Church as it settles in a new culture and confronts a different universe of meaning, Dumont describes the crisis of faith produced in Quebec by the political modernization produced by the Quiet Revolution:

> People of my age in Quebec have experienced a similar change of religious consciousness. We had received the faith from the family tradition and almost unanimous cultural practices; as we grew up, we had an inkling of the universal dimension of the Church, larger than the home and the parish, yet still in unbroken continuity. Then came the religious crisis, the public protests and the disaffection of a great number. Needed now was to move beyond the traditions, without denying them, to arrive at a historical consciousness of the faith.[9]

Crises of this kind, Dumont holds, are part of the history of salvation: they were experienced by the people of Israel when historical events radically altered their circumstances, such as the Babylonian exile and the return to Jerusalem. Such crises were also experienced by the Church as it moved into a new cultural environment. Quebecers living in the new Quebec, our author argues, had to move beyond the Catholicism of yesterday that had controlled their society. Quebec Catholics now reread the Scriptures, listen anew to the biblical figures, critically rethink their history, and seek a divine message in response to the growing unbelief in their society. Reflecting on the cloud of witnesses, past and present, Quebecers may find memories and hope that allow them to remain believers, this time not by obedience to rules, but by appealing to *la ré-férence*, the symbolic identification with the Tradition with a capital T. Trusting the Gospel and the witnesses throughout the ages, believers become joyful Catholics, even if they have reservations regarding the contemporary magisterium and disagree with the pastoral policies of the Vatican.

The historical consciousness of theologians depends in part on the scientific study of history. Relying on the criteria of their discipline, historians arrive at the conclusion that many events recorded in Scripture and ecclesiastical documents did not really happen. Such events may turn out to be "myths," i.e., stories with a powerful religious meaning. Some believers find such scientific discoveries disturbing. Dumont recognizes that the positivistic presuppositions that dominate contemporary culture persuade people to dismiss myths as fables or fairy tales without any basis in reality. Yet as an anthropologist, Dumont recognizes that the meaning of imaginative stories can have a profound impact on people's personal consciousness and their collective identity, and in this manner affect the making of history. It is unscientific, he argues, to dismiss the myths mediated by religion and culture as unreal. Theologians will assign priority to the spiritual meaning of biblical and post-biblical events, leaving the question of their factuality to the historian. "Les traditions ne sont pas rendues caduques par l'émergence d'une conscience historique de la foi. Elles en sont rajeunies."[10]

As an example, Dumont mentions the figure of Abraham, the man of great faith, whose image has sustained the self-understanding and dedication of Jews, Christians, and Muslims through the ages, even if his historical existence has never been demonstrated. Truth, including divine truth, can be made known in different ways, through ideas, myths, poetry, gestures of love, symbols, and personal sacrifice. The Second Vatican Council acknowledged this.[11] In the Scriptures, we read, "truth is proposed and expressed in a variety of ways, depending on whether a text is history of one kind or another, or whether its form is that of prophecy, poetry, or another type of speech."[12]

Dumont recognizes that the historical consciousness of the contemporary theologian raises difficult pastoral problems. Should the preacher tell the congregation that certain biblical stories that in the past were regarded as historical, are now seen by theologians as myths? The Christmas story, the birth of Jesus in Bethlehem, recorded in the Gospels of Mathew and Luke, has become part of the Christian imagination. How will Catholics react when the preacher tells them that most contemporary biblical scholars do not regard these beautiful texts as historical accounts? They are read today as *midrash*, a literary form of Jewish rabbinical commentary that provides insights into matters hinted at in Bible. The Christmas story celebrates the birth of the messiah by weaving together messianic themes contained in the Hebrew Scriptures and other pious Jewish texts. For the believing community the story is therefore true in its own way, even if it does not correspond to factual history.

Dumont asks himself how the congregation will react to the results of the scientific exegesis. The matter-of-fact style of contemporary culture makes it difficult for people to understand religious discourse. At one point our author suggests that because the myths are true in their own way, there is no need to introduce the parishioners to their non-factuality. To illuminate the disconnection between culture and religion, our author introduces the distinction between the denotation and the connotation of words. The denotation of words refers to concrete objects: "bread" refers to this baked loaf and "table" refers to this piece of furniture. By contrast, the connotation of words communicates a certain feeling and brings to mind a set of associations. "Bread" here suggests warm, freshly baked bread, or food for the poor, or nourishment of the soul, including the bread of life. "Table" here suggests a table laid for supper or a common meal with friends or a banquet for many guests, including the Eucharistic table. Our author argues that the impact of science and technology has reduced the dominant discourse to denotation to such an extent that people no longer understand poetic or religious discourse, both of which rely on the connotation of words. People in today's world seem to prefer a literalist reading of biblical texts: the majority turns to secularism, while a minority surrenders to fundamentalism. The discovery that many biblical and post-biblical stories are not factual is a deeply disturbing experience for many Christians. Dumont acknowledges this. He recognizes that to acknowledge the truth implicit in myth and its power to transform human life is difficult for people affected by the matter-of-fact style of contemporary discourse. Yet he does not raise the question of whether the resistance to contemporary biblical scholarship is one of the reasons for the conservative movement in the Churches at this time. The books written by Joseph Ratzinger / Benedict XVI on the life and teaching of Jesus based on the four canonical Gospels[13] dismiss the historical-critical method in favour of a more literalist reading of the biblical texts. In his writings, Dumont pays no attention to the conservative current in contemporary Catholicism. He is firmly convinced that if the Church has a future in our society, it will be mediated by a critical openness to modernity.

5

The Theologian and the Critique of Culture

The neo-scholastic theology taught in Catholic faculties and seminaries did not include critical dialogue with the culture in which the Church found itself. Theology was looked upon as universally valid, the same in Rome, in European countries, and on other continents, unrelated to the distinct cultural environment and indifferent to the economic and political problems experienced by society. Because this theology did not demand listening to the present, nor rethinking its inheritance, Dumont refers to it as "automatic theology." It provided answers to questions people did not ask. Relying on nineteenth-century Catholic social thought, Leo XIII wrote the encyclical *Rerum Novarum* in 1891 that offered a critical analysis of industrial society and deplored the human damage produced by liberal capitalism. Yet this Catholic social teaching was not part of theology: it was based, not on biblical revelation, but on rational arguments following a particular interpretation of the natural law. Catholic social teaching became theologically grounded only in John XXIII's encyclical *Pacem in Terris* of 1963, which offered scriptural support for human rights and freedoms.[1] Because men and women were created in the image of God and redeemed by Jesus Christ, they have a high dignity, an entitlement to freedom that must be respected by governments and the laws of society. After

John XXIII, Catholic social teaching continued to invoke divine revelation and thus became a theological social ethics. While Catholic social teaching evolved, so did Catholic theology. An increasing number of theologians produced a contextual theology – that is to say, a theology addressing the truth and values of the culture to which it belongs. The need for contextual theology was recognized by the Second Vatican Council. The constitution *Gaudium et Spes* urges theologians to enter into dialogue with their culture, critique its dehumanizing potential, appreciate its achievements, and provide an articulation of the Gospel that can be understood by people in that culture and addresses their concrete problems and aspirations, "For thus the ability to express Christ's message in its own way is developed in each nation."[2] In each nation, in each context, the task of theology includes the critique of the culture to which it belongs.

Beginning with the Quiet Revolution, theology in Quebec became increasingly contextual. In the 1960s, Catholic theologians participated in the effort of the emerging Quebec nation to invent a new discourse in which to express its collective aspirations, until then largely buried.[3] Theologians asked themselves what the Gospel had to say to the people of Quebec as they recognized themselves as a nation, redefined their identity, and discovered their cultural creativity. In those years Dumont was associated with the Dominican review *Maintenant* and a circle of militant Catholics who offered theological arguments in support of the Quiet Revolution. With them Dumont favoured democratic socialism, which would entail a government that distributed the wealth of society and funded public education, scientific research, and the flourishing of the arts. Implicit in Dumont's social engagement was a liberal-socialist reading of modernity, seeing it as the collective enterprise of people struggling for freedom, justice, participation, and equality. With other critical Quebecers, Dumont denounced Quebec's political conservatism under premier Maurice Duplessis († 1959) and his reactionary, anti-labour, and undemocratic policies. In his articles at this time, Dumont wrote as a socialist critical of the dominant free-market economy and as a nationalist deeply attached to his cultural roots.

In the early 1980s, as economic and cultural neo-liberalism was spreading in his society, Dumont, deeply disappointed, has hardly anything good to say of Quebec society. In his *L'institution de la théologie* he laments the turn to the superficial life, indifferent to values, devoid of ideals, detached from the inherited culture, oriented toward consumerism, and obsessed with the desire for wealth. He complains of the "de-culturation" of society. He argues that the government no longer respects the values and vision of the Quiet Revolution, that powerful corporations impose their policies upon the people without attention to their well-being, and that society as a whole has become an inflexible system that frustrates the majority and that nobody knows how to change. In his chapter 5 on the theologian and the critique of culture, Dumont replaces the liberal-socialist reading of modernity he endorsed in the 1960s by the dark analysis of contemporary society, in line with the critical thought of Max Weber.

Dumont has written a great deal about the critical dialogue of theology with culture. Even his secular books contain sections dealing with the role religion could or should play in society. His articles on this topic published in reviews and collections have as yet not been collected in a single volume. It would be a worthwhile undertaking to analyze in detail the evolution of Dumont's ideas on the dialogue of theology with culture. His chapter 5 of *L'institution de la théologie* offers only a narrow slice of his social thought.

THE BUREAUCRATIZATION OF SOCIETY

Dumont begins chapter 5 with an analysis of the bureaucratization of contemporary society. He recalls that in traditional societies, most people live in small communities that provide the rules and guide the practices that assure a peaceful *vivre ensemble*. The small communities also produce the food, the goods, and the shelter the people need. The king or emperor that rules the land does not interfere in the life of these communities, as long as they pay their taxes. This situation changes radically when the rational planning of the modern State interferes in the life of the communities, interrupts their customs, introduces universal legislation, and imposes a central authority. The State now becomes the bureaucratic designer of society, paying little attention to the experiences of the people.

During the Quiet Revolution Dumont offered a more positive evaluation of the State: he fully approved of government support for welfare, education, healthcare, scientific research, and cultural development. He hoped that Quebec would become a participatory society, planned by government in dialogue with the people and their institutions. Yet this did not happen.

The trend towards bureaucratization, Dumont now argues in chapter 5, has been operative in the economy as well. In traditional society, economic production is local: it is an activity that provides the goods needed by the community, produces lasting personal relations, and strengthens the social bond assuring the unity of society. Yet as new technology dramatically increases the production of goods, the new economy provides commodities for sale at home and abroad and leads to the accumulation of private wealth. The new economy, leaving the local communities, is taken over by large, privately owned industries and commercial companies and steered by their owners to increase their own profit. Modern economic corporations have become giant bureaucracies, unconcerned about the well-being of society and its population.

Another example of the bureaucratization of society, Dumont proposes in chapter 5, is the creation of a universal school system. The schools set up by towns, guilds, parishes, and monasteries in the past were now replaced by the public education of young people, following a curriculum devised by the State for the entire nation, without attention to local concerns. We recall that in the 1960s, the young Dumont fully supported Quebec's new educational system devised by the Parent Commission. Now, in the 1980s, Dumont argues that the schools controlled by the State tend to reduce young people to the roles they must play in society: they are citizens, clients, workers, managers, customers, employees, teachers, or students, with clearly defined tasks and duties, gradually making them disappear as human beings. The bureaucratization of society has damaged the *humanum*. Dumont even accuses the social sciences of studying only the roles people play in their society, paying no attention to the people themselves with their own experiences and aspirations.

Recalling the three ways of being members of a community described in chapter 3,[4] Dumont now proposes that in traditional societies most people were members of a community by "belonging," while in the modern society most people are members by "integration." Our author argues that the trend towards bureaucratization and integration has also been operative in the Catholic Church, a process that undermines its spiritual vitality and threatens its survival in many places.

Dumont does not refer to Max Weber's writings on bureaucracy, nor does he mention Weber's prediction that the ongoing "rationalization" of institutional life, driven by trust in scientific planning, will transform society into "an iron cage," fully administered, without beauty and passion, painted grey upon gray.[5] To offer support for his dark analysis, Dumont quotes the famous text from Tocqueville's *Democracy in America* that envisages democracy turning into a new form of despotism:

The first thing that strikes the observation is an innumerable multitude of men, all equal and alike, incessantly endeavoring to procure the petty and paltry pleasures with which they glut their lives. Each of them, living apart, is as a stranger to the fate of all the rest; his children and his private friends constitute to him the whole of mankind. As for the rest of his fellow citizens, he is close to them, but he does not see them; he touches them, but he does not feel them; he exists only in himself and for himself alone; and if his kindred still remain to him, he may be said at any rate to have lost his country.

Above this race of men stands an immense and tutelary power, which takes upon itself alone to secure their gratifications and to watch over their fate. That power is absolute, minute, regular, provident, and mild. It would be like the authority of a parent if, like that authority, its object was to prepare men for manhood; but it seeks, on the contrary, to keep them in perpetual childhood: it is well content that the people should rejoice, provided they think of nothing but rejoicing. For their happiness such a government willingly labors, but it chooses to be the sole agent and the only arbiter of that happiness; it provides for their security, foresees and supplies their necessities, facilitates their pleasures, manages their principal concerns, directs their industry, regulates the descent of property, and subdivides their inheritances: what remains, but to spare them all the care of thinking and all the trouble of living?[6]

"Tocqueville était un bon prophète," Dumont writes. Yet our author fails to mention that in this book Tocqueville praises the humane values fostered by democracy in America; he wanted to persuade his aristocratic friends in France that equality of citizenship does not necessarily lead to instability and social chaos. While he admits the possibility that democracy might turn into a new form of dictatorship, Tocqueville describes in great detail the features of American political and cultural life that are likely to prevent this from happening.

In his chapter 5 Dumont offers a dark analysis of modern
society, including his own beloved Quebec, that does not take
into account the ideas of his that are expressed and explored
in other writings. In chapter 5 he focuses exclusively on the
dehumanizing impact of the bureaucratizing process. He argues that the bureaucratic organization of social life on every
level fails to respect people's values, their self-understanding,
or their social commitment. Abolishing their co-responsibility
for society and disregarding their concern for the common
good, the intense bureaucratization produces self-involved individuals, concerned with nothing but themselves. While every
culture is in crisis – we have explained this idea of Dumont
above – the present crisis, Dumont now argues, is altogether
special because the new individualism undermines the institutions and associations that sustain the social order, such as the
family, the parish, the local community, the labour union, and
the political party. People now feel free to do whatever pleases
them. They seek quick satisfaction and become eager consum-
ers, habits that prevent them from inwardness and social engagement. To self-involved individuals, society appears like a
giant shopping centre where the rich can buy what they want
and the poor can look at the goods they desire. Here human
life knows no moments of self-transcendence.

ALTERNATIVE CULTURAL PROJECTS

I am puzzled by Dumont's critical social analysis in chapter 5.
Selfish individualism is denounced by conservatives as well as
thinkers of the left. Conservatives lament people's loss of
rootedness in their inherited social institutions, while the left-
wing critics bemoan the decline of social solidarity and people's unwillingness to join the struggle for social justice. In his
chapter 5, Dumont opts for the conservative critique of society, without mentioning the inequalities produced by capitalist society. I find this puzzling because in other writings, our
author presents himself as a socialist. In *La vigile du Québec*

(1971), the only book of Dumont's translated into English, he has an entire chapter on the appropriate form of socialism for Quebec society.[7] He writes, "For a society such as ours, tormented by the vulnerability of its material condition and a consciousness incapable of fostering its development, socialism is the one option in continuity with its destiny and its vision of the future."[8] In a chapter of his *Raisons communes*, published in 1995, eight years after *L'institution de la théologie*, Dumont analyzes at great length the inequalities of Quebec society, revealing himself deeply troubled by the high level of unemployment and the exclusion of the poor and various other groups assigned to the margin.[9]

Dumont's critical social analysis in chapter 5 is also puzzling because it does not refer to a basic idea of his, the vulnerability of every culture. Even the neo-liberal culture that has come to dominate Quebec society has the inherent potential of being split open by frustrated citizens (*le dédoublement*) and giving rise to the creation of an alternative culture. Dumont recognizes this in other books: frustration with the bureaucratized society produces alternative cultural projects. Here are two paragraphs:

> Significant is the multiplication of parallel cultures. The Churches are challenged from within or without by sects and small communities. The extensive medical system finds itself accompanied by popular groups offering health services. In the margin of the official networks of literature, art and information spring up alternative centers of production.
>
> This decline of support for the big institutions favours the growth and expansions of new forms of power. As the political, religious and scientific organizations multiply and expand their institutions, they are actually losing the power they had. An ever increasing gap occurs between the culture of managers and executives and the culture of the human community.[10]

In his *Raisons communes* Dumont expresses his esteem for *le mouvement communautaire* (community development) and the social economy in Quebec.[11] He thinks that the productive social interactions that characterize the neighbourhood today prolong in some sense the vitality of the local parish. People give up their religious practice, yet remain inclined to form communities, volunteer to help their neighbours, and set up self-help groups and cooperatives. For Dumont, this is a case of "rupture" and "fidelity." He writes, "In my opinion, we have here the greatest social innovation of the last decades."[12] Yet in chapter 5 there is not a word about the impressive creativity of community development and the social economy in Quebec society, a phenomenon that has since become recognized worldwide.[13] In *Raisons communes*, Dumont writes,

> The welfare state continues to appeal, but as the politicians glorify on all platforms the importance of the economy and the market society, the collectivity of Quebec, having been shaken in its foundation, is actually reconstructing itself from the bottom up . As the utopias of the classless society have not led to anything, the utopia of community development is gaining ground, albeit discreetly.[14]

Dumont does not think for a moment that a social movement from the bottom up can, by itself, transform the capitalist economy, yet he recognizes the potential of *le mouvement communautaire* and the social economy to promote an alternative culture in Quebec that may eventually lead to the creation of a more just society.

Dumont did not foresee, nor did any sociologist anticipate, that in February 2012 tens of thousands of students of Quebec universities and colleges, frustrated by the bureaucratization of society and the spread of free-market individualism, would start a well-organized protest movement that, at first, objected to the government's decision to raise university fees and that, eventually, became a widely supported oppositional movement against the imposition of the market model on the conduct of universities and other public institutions. Remembering the social values of the Quiet Revolution, such as freedom, solidarity, equality, and transparency, the students asked for a public debate on the nature of Quebec society and the role of education and culture within it. The report of the Parent Commission in 1963–64 had recommended public support for education, including university studies. While the government believed the issue had simply to do with money, the students recognized that the cost of university education is related to the self-understanding of society. Why is it that in English-speaking countries university fees are high, while in most European countries university education is free or at a low cost? The issue to be debated, the students argued, is social philosophy.

The mobilization of tens of thousands of students in Quebec confirms what Fernand Dumont has written about the vulnerability of the dominant culture to le dédoublement, yet this massive protest contradicts the deterministic reading of society in his chapter 5.

SELFISH INDIVIDUALISM

In chapter 5 Dumont focuses exclusively on two dark phenomena of contemporary society: the rigid bureaucratization of institutions that exclude people from any participation and the empty individualism that undermines their social concern and trivializes the spiritual life. He then offers, as we shall see, his own theological responses to these two troubling events. By contrast, a good many Quebec theologians base their theological reflections on the alternative social movements, the creative aspect of contemporary society. This is done, for instance, by the authors of *L'utopie de la solidarité au Québec*,[15] who are greatly impressed by the creativity at the community level of society. While these authors do not accept Dumont's

dark social analysis of chapter 5, they follow Dumont's theological method: responding to concrete events, they reread the
Scriptures and rethink their history to find memories and
signs of hope that support their engagement for compassion
and social justice.

Deeply troubled by the culture of selfish individualism,
Dumont wonders whether the preoccupation with one's own
life has been encouraged by the Christian preaching of the
salvation of the soul. While the message of the Old Testament
deals principally with fidelity to the Covenant and the commitment to social justice of God's first-chosen people, the
message of the New Testament, Dumont argues, lends itself
to an individualistic interpretation focusing on the salvation
of souls. There have been and still are spiritual currents in
Christianity, Dumont argues, that foster a purely private piety
and concentrate on personal salvation, while the main emphasis of the Catholic tradition, he insists, is on the redemp-
tion of the believing community and its mission in the world.
Still, he fears that the pressure of the dominant culture may
push Catholics into the trap of empty individualism. Following
the American sociologist Peter Berger, Dumont thinks that the
Church's openness to ecumenism and the world religions
may lead to the polite acceptance of religious pluralism and
prompt Catholics to move from the commitment to one truth
to the acknowledgment of many ways to God. Are we confronted here, Dumont asks, with something like a religious
market where people choose the religion that suits them
at a particular moment? If religion becomes an object of
consumption, he continues, it is no longer able to mediate
Transcendence to the present generation. "From now on it
no longer suffices to proclaim with Vatican II the freedom
of conscience. How can one commit one's conscience when a
religious belief has become a commodity?"[16]

I am again puzzled by this dark interpretation. To oppose
faith in the Gospel, the one great truth, to the respectful appreciation of other religious traditions is a reactionary stance

that does not fit into Dumont's theology. Since religious con-
flicts continue to produce hostility and even acts of violence
in some parts of the world, the contemporary effort to recon-
cile the world religions in mutual respect, cooperation, and
spiritual communion is a redemptive event, unique in world
history, an unmerited divine gift, even if the Churches have
not yet found an adequate theological justification for it. As
Dumont constantly emphasizes, the faith experience of believers and their community precedes theological formulations and doctrinal definitions.

TWO CREATIVE THEOLOGICAL RESPONSES

In his chapter 5 Dumont offers theological responses to the
two dehumanizing phenomena mentioned by him: (1) the
rigid bureaucratization of society and (2) the spread of selfish
individualism.

The Bureaucratization of Society

To counter the bureaucratization of institutions, Dumont
turns to the Political Theology of Johann Baptist Metz[17] that
envisaged the Church of the future as a prophetic community,
critical of the dehumanizing ideas and mechanisms operative
in contemporary society. Dumont interprets Metz's proposal
as the request that the Church reflect critically on its own self-
organization, admit that it has also become bureaucratized
and alienating, and invent alternative institutional forms that
reflect more clearly the preaching of Jesus and the working of
the Holy Spirit. Because the Church has become worldly, multiplying its doctrines, laws, and regulations without listening
to the faith experience of the people, its presence in society
offers no saving message. The Church's task is to create institutional forms in keeping with the self-understanding of the
believing community, based on God's Word. I recall that the
Dumont Report published in 1971 insisted on the need for

institutions in the Church that facilitate dialogue between the authorities and the believing community. A society sins against human dignity if it provides no institution that allows people to engage in constructive conversation with their leaders. Dumont now argues that if the Church were to conduct its institutional life in the spirit of the Gospel, it would render a prophetic testimony, challenge the bureaucratization of society, and help to summon forth an alternative public culture.

Dumont's proposal corresponds to the emphasis made in his chapter 3 on the importance of witnessing. Witnessing is more credible than mere words. The Church's teaching on justice, cooperation, and solidarity becomes credible when the Church as an institution practices these virtues. Dumont's proposal also corresponds to his analysis of membership in the Church. Instead of promoting membership by "integration," the ecclesiastical authorities should foster membership by "reference" or symbolic identification with the events of salvation and the faith witnesses throughout the ages. Instead of insisting on unanimity in matters not central to the Gospel, the magisterium should confirm by its own witness the memories, symbols, and testimonies that constitute the religious identity of the Catholic community. Such an emphasis on the collective identity would leave room for internal pluralism and respect the consciences of believers.

Metz's Political Theology proposed that the Church be prophetic also by denouncing the unjust structures and practices of society. Fernand Dumont shared this conviction. I think he was in full agreement with the vision of the future Church proposed by Jacques Grand'Maison, a close friend of his, a vision I have summarized as follows:

The Church of the future, in Quebec and in the industrialized world in general, [will be] a relatively small community, no longer identified with an entire nation, no longer a *Volkskirche* as the Germans call it, but representing a creative minority in society which, thanks to the power of the Gospel, has an impact far beyond its borders. The Church will become prophet: its communal life will address a critical message to society. The Church of the future ... will be humble, admit that it does not have all the answers, welcome the creativity of the faithful, and be open to all who believe in Christ, without discrimination. The humble Church will symbolize in a more credible way the figure of Jesus, the loving yet demanding prophet in whom God's Word has become incarnate in human history.[18]

The Spread of Selfish Individualism

To counter vacant individualism, theologians will have to uncover the deep root of subjectivity, the fine point where persons are subject to the Holy Spirit. Another surprise of chapter 5 is that the alternative to selfish individualism which Dumont proposes here is not Emmanuel Mounier's personalism, which our author praises and endorses in other writings.[19] For Mounier, individuals, far from being detached and empty, are persons originating in community, participating in its vision and values, and acquiring a moral conscience urging them to assume responsibility for society. In one form or another, personalist philosophy has been widely accepted in Catholic theological schools and left an imprint on the Second Vatican Council. In *Gaudium et Spes* (#55) we read, "Thus we are witnesses of the birth of a new humanism, one in which man is defined first of all by this responsibility to his brothers (and sisters) and to history."

In chapter 5, Dumont does not try to correct the pervasive empty individualism by the carefully balanced anthropology of personalism, combining as it does personal freedom and social commitment. Opting for a more radical remedy, our author quotes Gabriel Marcel: "Private life and it alone provides the mirror in which the Infinite deigns to reflect itself: personal relations and they alone point to a personality situated beyond our daily perspectives."[20] Dumont agrees that the entry into truth happens in the heart; and if it does not happen in the heart, it will not happen at all. Calling individuals to enter into their spiritual interior has been done by mystics throughout the ages and by passionate religious thinkers such as Pascal and Kierkegaard. If people caught in empty individualism seek to escape their condition by turning to social engagement – as a personalist philosopher might suggest – they will find no rescue. They shall remain ignorant of their own depth, Dumont thinks, and thus be unable to encounter the transcendent source of life that alone could empower them to become witnesses of faith and engage in the renewal of society.

It follows from these two reflections that the theologian critical of contemporary culture must be committed to two orientations, the prophetic and the mystical, both giving witness to divine transcendence. Dumont dismisses the distinction often made today between spirituality (which is welcome) and religion (which is outmoded). A spirituality that finds no institutional expression, he argues, leaves the world to its immanence, deprived of a summons to transcend its present condition. As we have seen, Dumont recognizes an internal dynamics in the lives of human beings making them restless and orienting them towards an inexpressible Transcendence. Dumont offers a similar argument for society. Thanks to the critical aspirations of its citizens, society sees itself as incomplete and unfinished, forever called to reform itself and become more humane, summoned by a hidden Transcendence, an unreachable and indescribable Other that nonetheless has an impact on history. Dumont insists on this point even in his secular writings.

His *Raisons communes*, published in 1995, offers a set of proposals that outline how Quebecers, now deeply divided, could find a common ground to renew their society. In a section entitled "institution et transcendence," he writes,

In order to have a public space where the freedom of some does not repress the freedom of others and where people support the common good to which all have access without making excessive claims, important work must be done by the nation, the State and the law. Each component of a society that is alive must be open to transcendence and closed to self-regard. All public institutions have two sides: they are existing organizations with their proper purpose, and they represent at the same time the as yet unfinished community, a building site as it were, the place and the means of a cooperative effort. Nothing is assured ahead in this twofold undertaking.[21]

Dumont concludes that society remains alive and non-repressive only if it is open to Transcendence – not a transcendence above the community, but one that is immanent in its substance. Without the openness to Transcendence, society will turn its vision and values into a fixed ideology, sacralize its practices, and see itself as a manifestation of the absolute. Without the openness to Transcendence, society will become an idol.

The theologian critical of contemporary culture must have the courage to challenge the closure of society upon itself and uphold the importance of giving practical recognition of Transcendence. The theologian, Dumont argues, will not urge the Christian faith upon society; all he or she will do is to articulate the liberating presence of a transcendent power that rescues society from its ideological and idolatrous self-understanding.

Dumont, as we have mentioned before, does not want to reconvert Quebec society to the Catholic faith. He has great respect for his non-believing friends and colleagues. He makes a clear distinction between atheists and agnostics. Atheists, unpuzzled by the mystery of life, deny God's existence, while agnostics, aware of the unresolved questions posed by the universe, are unable to believe in God. Agnostics may well have an implicit faith in Transcendence without a name that saves them from ideology and idolatry.[22] The anxiety they experience, Dumont thinks, is similar to the anxiety of Christian believers who continue to ask questions for which there are no final answers. The theologian critical of contemporary culture should foster dialogue with non-believers about the ethical summons implicit in their society.

BEYOND RELATIVISM

While Dumont does not raise the issue of relativism in chapter 5, he refers to it in other writings. Since the sociology of knowledge holds that ideas and values are always expressions of a particular cultural context, some social scientists argue that each society has its own wisdom and that there are no universal truths and no universal ethical principles. Their position can be read as an ethical relativism, a denial of a universal, context-transcending idea of the good, dissolving the hope that today's deeply divided humanity can ever be reconciled in a just and peaceful world community. Relativism has dangerous political implications. Many years ago, I studied three German scholars who applied the sociology of knowledge in their work – Ernst Tröltsch, Max Scheler, and Karl Mannheim; they were all passionately opposed to relativism.[23] If truth and values cannot unite the human family, then empires or dictators will feel justified in trying to unite the world by force. Each of these scholars tried to transcend relativism in his own way. Each recognized in the diverse cultures a universal dimension that made possible the emergence of an ethical consensus. Dumont follows the same path. The key to his refutation of relativism, as we shall see, is his distinction between "the general" and "the universal."

For Dumont, we note, truth and values are not added to society from the outside. They belong to the substance of society: a stable cooperative existence implies a set of common values, such as trust, veracity, justice, and solidarity. These values take different forms in the different societies. The concrete ethical norms differ from one society to another. For this reason, no society may present its own values as "general," i.e., as valid in all parts of the world. To "generalize" the norms of one's own culture or community, Dumont argues, constitutes a form of absolutism. At the same time, he holds that the diverse cultures, all being human, have the capacity to be open to one another, engage in respectful dialogue, appreciate their difference, and, in acting together, generate a common ethics. Cultural traditions are dynamic historical realities, enlivened by the internal debate among their members and an ongoing contact with other cultures. The vital power of cultural traditions allows them to respond creatively to historical challenges by rethinking their ideas and values and reforming their customs and practices.[24] While each culture must refuse to "generalize" its norms, it is able to discern in them universal principles, such as truth, justice, and solidarity – principles whose concrete definition differs from one culture to another. Dumont's distinction between "the general" and "the universal" allows him to reject the generalization of norms and avoid absolutism, and at the same time affirm the universality implicit in these norms and avoid relativism. Dialogue and cooperation in response to a common historical challenge are capable of generating a common ethics, and if such interaction involves all societies of the globe, there may well emerge a universal ethical consensus, respectful of cultural differences.

I was struck by the similarity between Dumont's sense of the universal and the idea of pluralism developed by Johann Gottfried Herder (1744–1803). Reacting to the generalization of reason proposed by many thinkers of the Enlightenment, Herder insisted on the plurality of languages and cultures, each with its own understanding of the true and the good – an idea that later persuaded many social scientists to accept relativism. Herder himself believed that the different cultures were capable of opening themselves to one another, participating in the same historical movement, and aspiring to a common humane ethos (*Humanität*).²⁵ He saw in the great variety of cultures different versions of the Golden Rule, a striving for mutuality and respect, and a search for values that promoted the well-being of all. Because Herder's nationalism has often been accused of producing contempt for outsiders, I wish to cite the following quotation:

> It is the apparent plan of nature that as one human being … and one nationality learn, learn incessantly, from and with the others, until all have comprehended the difficult lesson that no nationality has been solely designated by God as the chosen people of the earth; above all we must seek the truth and cultivate the garden of the common good. Hence no nationality of Europe may separate itself sharply, and foolishly say, "With us alone, with us dwells all wisdom."²⁶

A concrete example of such an intercultural dialogue has been the experience of the World Conference of Religion for Peace, founded in 1970 when the world lived in fear of a possible nuclear exchange between the United States and the Soviet Union. Here dialogue among the representatives of the world religions allowed them to articulate common insights and common values, even though they came from very different cultures. At their meetings every four years, they were able to produce joint declarations on peace in the world. In the declaration made at Louvain in 1974, they admit that in the past their religious traditions have often blessed wars and supported unjust rulers, but they confess at the same time that the deepest and most authentic values of their traditions promote peace and justice. The participants in this meeting committed themselves to become active in the renewal of their own religious traditions, giving priority to the common values of peace and justice.²⁷

Pope Benedict XVI regards relativism as the great danger of modern culture, undermining all moral and religious convictions and making society vulnerable to oppression and domination. He has lamented "the dictatorship of relativism,"[28] but did not warn society of absolutism, which also threatens the peace of the world. In his book *Moral Relativism*, the American philosopher Steven Lukes accuses Benedict XVI of absolutism. Lukes quotes a sentence from the Instruction *Dominus Jesus*, published in 2000 by the Vatican Congregation of the Doctrine of the Faith, signed by its president Cardinal Ratzinger, asserting that religious pluralism exists only *in fact*, not *in principle*, for in principle there is only one religion, Roman Catholicism. In a theological statement of religious pluralism, the bishops of Quebec reject both relativism (assuming that all religions are equally true) and absolutism (assuming that there is no truth outside of one's own religion).[29] It deserves to be mentioned that on the issue of religious pluralism, Benedict XVI has changed his mind over the years. He now respects the diversity of religions, recognizes the urgency of interreligious dialogue, and envisages a peaceful *vivre ensemble* of the diverse religious communities.[30]

Fernand Dumont is not a relativist. At the same time, he does not use Pope Benedict's vehement rhetoric against relativism. Dumont's awareness of Transcendence in human history makes him feel that everything in the created order is relative. There is only one Absolute: the incomprehensible divine mystery. This is how I summarized Dumont's position in a previous paragraph: "Without the openness to Transcendence, society will turn its vision and values into a fixed ideology, sacralize its practices, and see itself as a manifestation of the absolute. Without the openness to transcendence, society will become an idol."

Chapter 5 on the theologian and the critique of culture contains many important ideas, but if my analysis is correct, it does not render a full account of Dumont's thought on this topic. Some of the proposals of chapter 5 differ from positions defended by Dumont in his other writings. The complexity of modern society and its ever-changing power relations make it impossible for a thoughtful critic to be fully consistent.

6

The Unity of Theology

Chapter 6 of *L'institution de la théologie* raises the question of the unity of theology – its unity as an intellectual discipline and its responsibility for promoting the unity of the believing community. In a subsequent section, Dumont proposes three ways of doing theology today, in Quebec and in modern society in general.

SCIENCE AND PHILOSOPHY

Dumont first raises the question of how one can speak of the unity of science and the unity of philosophy, despite the internal pluralism in both of these disciplines. He makes the following proposals.

What the sciences have in common is that they rely on the same methodology. They begin with simple observations, raise questions about what they observe, and produce answers that are rationally demonstrable. They use paradigms to organize their empirical observations and formulate theories that are universally valid. At the same time, their scientific constructs are tentative: they can be questioned by new observations and may demand the reorganization of the data using different paradigms. Because the new science builds upon the old, it is possible to speak of the progress of science. In applying the scientific method, the scientists are detached from their personal history and their social situation. They try to be what Dumont (following Piaget) calls "epistemic subjects," persons lifted out of their historical context in search of verifiable knowledge. While the scientist's detachment is never perfect, it represents an ideal. Scientists humbly present their scientific results to "the community of proof testers," i.e. the guild of scientists ready to check if the demonstrations are sound. The unity of scientific knowledge is achieved, Dumont writes, at a great price: the ascetical discipline of bracketing the life stories of the scientists and disregarding the concrete conditions of the society to which they belong.

Is it possible, Dumont asks, to speak of the unity of philosophy? Here thought reflects the personal experience of the thinker and the social context to which he or she belongs. For this reason, one cannot speak of the progress of philosophy. It is possible to define the unity of philosophy by the willingness of philosophers to respect one another, despite their differences, and by their openness to dialogue and rational arguments. What philosophers have in common is the search for a knowledge that sheds light on the unanswered questions implicit in human life and the cosmos. According to Dumont, "science achieves its unity in the demonstrable construct and the community of proof verifiers," while philosophy seeks its unity in "the anxiety implicit in being that summons forth a community of dialogue and self-questioning."[1]

THE UNITY OF THEOLOGY

The unity of theology is produced by its relation to God's self-revelation throughout the ages, even if this relation is at times obscure or hidden. Because theology depends on the historical context of the believing community, it is impossible to speak of the progress of theology, even if there is progress in some of its sub-disciplines, such as history or archaeology. What all Christian theologians have in common, and what they share with ordinary believers, is the Christian faith entailing repentance and gratitude. Theologians are united, Dumont adds, by experiencing the anxiety implicit in the mystery of being. Like scientists and philosophers, theologians also submit their work to a community of proof verifiers to check if the arguments used are reliable. Yet their work is essentially different from science and philosophy – a rupture preserving a certain continuity. While theologians often invoke scientific research and engage in dialogue with philosophy, theology itself is different from both, since it proceeds from a spiritual conversion and demands a commitment to a new practice.

What follows from the preceding chapters is that the theologian, in contrast to the philosopher, does not rely on the singularity of his or her own experience to gain insight into the universal human condition. The theologian listens to the experience of the believing community, follows the voice of the magisterium, remains faithful to the norms of Scripture and Tradition, and challenges the ambiguity of his or her own culture. As mediators committed to the service of the believing community, theologians do not leave the concern for the unity of faith simply to the magisterium; they consider promoting this unity also their own task.

FIRST AND SECOND THEOLOGY

It also follows that unlike philosophy, theology does not look upon the beliefs of people as the prejudices and fables of the unlearned. Theology listens respectfully to the faith of the people. Dumont insists that when ordinary Catholics reflect on what their faith means to them in the present, they actually engage in theology. This is especially true at this time when people are believers by personal conviction, and no longer by cultural inheritance. They practice what Dumont calls "first theology" or "first degree theology." He even puts the declarations of the magisterium into this category. Relying on scholarly research and dialogue with philosophy, the professional theologian practices "second theology" or "second degree theology." Yet the aim of academic theology is not to converse with the learned, nor to seek academic recognition, but to sustain and renew the faith of the believing community, to show the unity implicit in the rich diversity of Catholic religious experience, and to enhance the power of the community to give witness to the Gospel in the world.

In this context Dumont makes an observation regarding the modernist crisis under Pius X at the beginning of the twentieth century. This crisis was provoked by debates among theologians in search of a scientific approach to the Bible or engaged in an open dialogue with modern thought. These theologians still distinguished between the learned, the *maiores*, in search of verifiable insights, and the ordinary believers, the *minores*, heirs of a less enlightened faith. This was the reason why the theologians caught in the modernist crisis engaged in critical conversation only with one another, while omitting to speak with the faithful. Dumont thinks that this omission was a mistake: these theologians overlooked their call to be mediators.

Dumont does not mention that the theologians involved in the renewal movement that led to the Second Vatican Council were sensitive to the questions and aspiration of ordinary believers challenged by the secular culture in which they lived. They were pastorally concerned, they were mediators, and they wrestled with the political and cultural problems of their society.

Dumont insists at the same time that listening to the believing community does not dispense theologians from the critical task of challenging the dominant ideas. Our author quotes an observation made by the French Bishop Albert Rouet related to the definition of Mary's Immaculate Conception of 1855 and Mary's Bodily Assumption of 1955: both were largely based on the piety of the people, on their first degree theology. Rouet regrets that theologians did not speak to the people nor address the magisterium, showing them that the formulation of these redemptive events had problematic pastoral and cultural implications. The Immaculate Conception appears to encourage the fear of sin and cultural pessimism, and the Assumption assumes the dichotomy of body and soul – both implications that impede the saving impact of the Gospel on modern society.

In Quebec, women theologians have drawn attention to the ambiguity of the Marian piety that is part of the Catholic tradition.[2] It is possible to see Mary as fitting herself humbly and obediently into the institutions of patriarchy, leaving authority in the public order to males. Yet it is also possible to see her as the politicized woman of the Magnificat, asking God to push the princes from their thrones and raise high those of low degree (Lk 1:52).

Dumont raises the question whether the theology of the learned will scandalize believers in the parishes. At the time of the modernist crisis, the great majority of Catholics understood the stories told in Scripture as true in a literal sense, while in the present secular culture, Dumont argues, the great majority looks upon them as folklore or legends. It is thus high time that theologians and exegetes mediate the redemptive meaning of these tropes to the people in the parishes.

As mediators, Dumont argues, theologians are involved in a creative circle: first, they listen respectfully to the believing community; second, they test the multiple faith experiences with reference to Scripture, Tradition, and the magisterium; third, they critically examine the relation of these experiences to contemporary culture; fourth, they return again to the dialogue with the believing community.

Dumont worries that his attention to theology in chapter 6 might persuade the reader to think of the Gospel as a set of ideas and of faith as a series of concepts in the mind. Throughout his book, as we have seen, Dumont insists that divine revelation is constituted by events-and-words, and that this revelation continues to address the believing community. To hear this voice, theologians must attend to the concrete conditions of Church and society. Instead of referring exclusively to the ideal of the Church as one, holy, catholic, and apostolic, theologians will have to take into account the existing Church with its unresolved problems and contradictions. Since they see themselves as guardians of the Church's unity and protectors of the faith of the believing community, theologians may hesitate to expose and explore the dark side of the Church.

Dumont replies to this concern. Theologians, he suggests, must focus on God's redemptive work in human history – the economy of salvation, as the Church Fathers called it – which is testified in the Scriptures and present in the witnesses throughout the ages. The symbolic identification of believers with the economy of salvation (*la référence*) constitutes, as we have seen, the Catholic tradition. To strengthen people's Catholic faith there is no need to paint a faultless picture of the Catholic Church, nor to disguise its contradictions. To nourish and sustain the Catholic faith, spiritual leaders in the Church – bishops, priests, theologians, and teachers – must confirm *la référence*, the symbolic identification with redemptive events, past and present, in the Church and beyond the Church. Strengthening *la référence* is especially important, Dumont thinks, in periods of history when the magisterium, preoccupied with the defense of the Church as an institution, inclines to "ideologize" revealed truth and sacralize the existing church order. In my opinion, Dumont's observation is confirmed by the reaction of Catholics to the massive criminal sexual abuses committed by the clergy. To strengthen their faith, they do not focus on the hierarchical Church; they embrace instead the redemptive events in their own lives, in their community, in their Church, in society, right back through the history of witnesses to the life of Jesus Christ.

Let me explain at this point that when Fernand Dumont speaks of the Catholic Church, he does not intend to define it in contrast to the Protestant Churches. Catholicism, he writes, is the only version of Christianity which he knows well from personal experience and the study of history, yet he has great respect for what he has learnt of the Protestant tradition. Questioning the rationality behind the separation of the two Churches, he wonders whether the break has not been the product of ecclesiastical ideology. After all, what ordinary Christians wanted, Catholics as well as Protestants, was to live a life of faith, hope, and love. Yet they were given interpretative schemes that produced irreconcilable differences.

DOING THEOLOGY IN THREE WAYS

In his chapter 6, Dumont proposes three ways of doing theology: he refers to them as theology of mediation, theology of knowledge, and theology of interpretation. Yet he adds immediately that these three ways intersect and affect one another, suggesting that they constitute three dimensions of contemporary theology. If I understand him correctly, the first dimension is the awareness that theology serves proclamation, the second dimension is the exploration of the cognitive content of revelation, and the third dimension is the transformative impact of theology.

Toward a Theology of Mediation

To arrive at a theology of mediation, Dumont, following his usual method, offers first an analysis of mediation in a secular context. He recalls the dialectic of "experience," "expression," and "norm," described by him in chapter 2 and referred to by him in his entire anthropological work. Since his present topic is mediation or the communication of a message, he focuses on the expression of the experience, in French *le dire*, the putting of it into words. He admits that the expression may be a painting, a dance, or a piece of music, yet in this chapter on theology he pays attention to mediation in words. Mediation, he argues, involves an interpretation; it is partial; it does not exhaust the meaning of the experience. More importantly, mediation corresponds in some way to the mediator's concern and hence is relevant to him or her. Mediation is therefore not the articulation of a given, but a properly creative act. Saying it to oneself or to others is a new experience that in fact changes the mediator: it affects the way he or she sees the world and acts in it. Yet as the mediator acts differently and changes, he or she will review the initial experience and now interpret it differently. This to-and-fro between experience and expression is part of a dynamic, analyzed by Dumont in his anthropological studies, that makes thinking people discover both their finitude and their openness to Transcendence. In the present context, Dumont emphasizes that the mediation of experience, *le dire* or saying it, does not occur in concepts, but in figures or images that appeal to reason and the imagination.

Dumont's phenomenology of mediation is presented in an abstract manner, assuming the readers to be familiar with the philosophy developed in his published work. I wish to imagine a concrete illustration of his analysis by reflecting – in a hypothetical way – on the above-mentioned painful experience of Dumont's father. When he watched the horses as the halters were put on their necks, he suddenly recognized the slave existence imposed on him. He expressed his experience to his son in an image: I am a slave like these horses. He might then have felt the need to find criteria to check his experience, to prove to himself that he was not paranoid nor had reacted with undue self-pity. Then he might have spoken to other workers, shared his experience with them, and turning to some reading, recognized that he belonged to a movement, a labour movement struggling for justice. Telling his experience was a creative act; it opened his eyes and changed his self-understanding. It communicated a truth to his fellow workers that had been obscured, that was relevant to them, and that revealed them as human beings in need of liberation, a discovery with unending consequences.

Saying it is power; *le dire* transforms human life; uttering the message is action. This philosophical understanding of mediation has a surprising affinity with the biblical account of divine communication. Especially in the prologue to the fourth Gospel, the Word is powerful, the Word creates and redeems, the Word addresses all human beings. Among several other biblical texts, Dumont quotes, "The word of God is something alive and active; it cuts more incisively than any two-edged sword, it can seek out the place where soul is divided from sprit or joints from marrow, it can pass judgment on secret emotion and thoughts" (Heb 4:12). He quotes verses from the Book of Proverbs to show that the Wisdom of God speaks to the conscience of all, not just to members of the believing community. Instead of equating the Bible with the Word of God, Dumont affirms more precisely that God's Word can be heard in the Bible: to be addressed in power by the biblical text, one must be read it in the Spirit. Insensitive to the Spirit, literalist and fundamentalist readers of the Scriptures do not hear the Word.

Here again our author insists that divine revelation is constituted by events accompanied by words and communicated by stories and images – or figures– that continue to speak to the believing community as they move from one culture or one age to another. "These figures are the multiple voices of the economy of salvation that support the reading of the prophets and that the biblical authors, the theologians of the Bible, assemble and take over. These figures come together in Jesus, who is their Interpreter and their Fulfillment."[3] Divine revelation utters ever new messages to the believers, opening their eyes to what is happening in the world and in their hearts. Truth itself is a figure: it has many meanings, it transforms the believers' self-understanding, it is relevant to their lives and has an impact on their actions. Dumont respects the modern thinkers referred to as "masters of suspicion," such as Marx and Freud, because they disclose the destructive dimension hidden in common sense and the taken-for-granted perception of the world. God's prophetic Word, our author claims, does that too. Yet God's Word goes one step further: it reveals the ambiguity of our own hearts, our infidelities, the shadow of sin that we prefer to overlook.

Dumont's theology of mediation recognizes the power of God's Word in Scripture and the Church's proclamation. The Word creates and transforms. This is a theme greatly emphasized in the classical Protestant tradition. Catholics have reacted to this by insisting on the power of the sacraments: their impact is produced by the rite itself (*ex opere operato*). The words of proclamation are here seen as weak: they affect listeners only thanks to their own efforts (*ex opere operantis*). I remember that in preparation for the Second Vatican Council, the Secretariat of Christian Unity produced several draft documents for possible submission to the Council, among which was a theological statement on God's Word that retrieved the biblical and patristic teaching and sought to correct the one-sided Catholic emphasis on the sacraments. An ardent promoter of this statement was the German theologian Hermann Volk, a member of the Secretariat, subsequently the Cardinal Bishop of Mainz, committed to ecumenical dialogue with Lutheran Christians. While the statement was not chosen to be submitted to the Council, it was taken into account by the Theological Commission in the elaboration of *Dei Verbum*, the Constitution on Divine Revelation.

Fernand Dumont recognizes that God's Word is powerful. One task of theology, he thinks, is to serve the proclamation of the Word.

Toward a Theology of Knowledge

Dumont recognizes the need for a theology of knowledge, *une théologie de la connaissance*. Throughout the entire study, our author emphasizes that divine revelation is constituted by events plus words, expressed in figures, and may thus not be equated with a set of truths. At the same time, he refuses to overlook the cognitive content of divine revelation. Addressed and challenged by the figures of revelation, believers must seek a certain distance from them, question whether their reading is in keeping with the Bible as a whole and with the tradition of the witnesses, and in doing so clarify the concepts implicit in the stories of salvation. Reason in the basement, to use Dumont's image, poses questions and seeks answers. It prompts believers to explore the intelligibility of their faith. From the very beginning, a conversation in the believing community, guided by the magisterium, dealt with the question of who Jesus Christ is and how he is related to the God who sent him. Dumont writes,

> Christ is not a concept; he is a singular being to whom one commits one's faith in an act of charity that is not caught in a concept. At the same time it would be a concession to blind fideism not to raise questions about the identity of Jesus. From the beginning of the Church the great Christological debates assumed the task of finding answers to these questions relying on concepts and rational arguments.[4]

The questioning prompted by reason is the springboard of theology and reveals the necessary role played by theology in the Church. Dumont insists that theology cannot be replaced by the Scriptures, nor by the experience of the believing community, nor by the Church's official teaching and practice. It is the quest for knowledge, responding to God's Word mediated in figures, that founds and justifies theological inquiry. Theology is not limited to the pursuit of this knowledge. The theology of mediation, as we saw, clarifies the meaning of the revealed figures; and the theology of interpretation, as we shall see, deals with the transformative impact of these figures. Yet the theology of knowledge, produced by believers in dialogue with the wisdom of their age, presents the economy

of salvation as a philosophy or a worldview, capable of trans-
forming human self-understanding. Even though God's Word
is not a theory nor a collection of concepts, systematic theology occupies a necessary place in the Church – not by casting
divine revelation into a system, but by allowing believers to
clarify, for themselves and for their culture, the cognitive content implicit in God's self-revelation.

At the same time, our author insists that doctrine does not
save. Orthodoxy does not communicate the experience of
faith. What counts is the trusting response to God's Word
and the symbolic identification with the history of salvation
recorded in Scripture and witnessed in Tradition. In the perspective of faith, the opposite of truth is not error – error is
a human failing that in one way or another happens to everyone; the opposite of the truth is the lies that we tell ourselves and others – we as individuals and as collectivities.
Even the Church produces an ideology to legitimate its institutional presence which at times disguises the biblical
message. From all these untruths, God's Word intends to
deliver us.

While God's Word is transformative, it is also disclosure,
enlightenment, an utterance of hidden truth. Responding to
this enlightenment, the human mind moves beyond the figures and the redemptive experiences to expressions of objectivity founded upon rational arguments. Knowledge is based
on evidence that can be tested by all and makes use of concepts that are familiar to all. The great temptation has been,
Dumont argues, to generalize these concepts, i.e., to regard
them as valid and appropriate in all parts of the world.
Theologians have often refused to recognize the plurality of
cultures and to admit that the concepts on which they rely
may have no meaning outside of their own cultural context.
The theology of knowledge will always be richly pluralistic,
different from one culture to another, in each context using
concepts derived from its own cultural inheritance.

Dumont here recalls the above-mentioned distinction between the general and the universal.[5] God's Word as enlightenment constitutes one universally valid truth, yet the theological efforts to clarify the ideas implicit in this truth will be many, depending upon the historical situation of the believing community. If the Church obliges theologians to rely on philosophical concepts of the past, Dumont warns, its teaching is likely to become incomprehensible to the people in today's society. Theologians need to be in dialogue with the intellectual life in their own culture, trusting that theologians situated in other cultures will do the same. The Church has a common creed expressed in broad terms and recited in the liturgical worship, yet the theological understanding of what the articles of the creed mean may well differ from one culture to another. Does this theological pluralism, Dumont asks himself, undermine the unity of the Church?

Since all cultures are human, Dumont replies to his own question, they are open to one another: cross-cultural dialogue is possible. Moreover, since theologians of different cultures practice dialogue with one another and participate in a common worship, they are able to understand one another, expand their horizons, and affirm in their own way the great truth they hold in common. The theological pluralism in the Church, Dumont argues, is in principle reconcilable and is in fact oriented towards the unity of faith.

Toward a Theology of Interpretation

Interpretation is constantly at work in theology. The theology of mediation interprets the revealed figures as a service to proclamation, and the theology of knowledge interprets these figures to clarify their cognitive contents in a particular culture. The theology of interpretation is defined by Dumont as the spiritual effort of theologians to hear in God's Word answers to the unresolved questions that trouble the conscience of the believing community. Interpretation renders the Gospel relevant to a particular historical context.

During the Hitler regime and the persecution of the Jews, the courageous German New Testament scholar Erik Peterson proposed that in order to make the doctrine of Christ's two natures, divine and human, relevant to the German context, the Church should profess Christ's two natures as divine and Jewish. Yet no one followed his suggestion.

The relation of truth and relevance is a major issue in Dumont's philosophical work. He argues at length against the presumptions of positivism often taken for granted in university departments of the natural and human sciences. The scientists in these departments regard the quest for knowledge as a purely objective project, detached from their own personal concerns and the problems of their society. In Dumont's terminology, they try to be "epistemic subjects," value-free knowledge-seekers withdrawn from the moral challenges of their time. While an objectivity of this kind is their ideal, scientists recognize that they are unable to realize it completely.

We have seen that Dumont has an entirely different understanding of human knowledge. *Le croire*, or believing, is always prior to knowledge. We receive the light in which we see the world from our culture. The scholars who claim to be value-neutral ignore the extent to which their perspective has been mediated by the dominant culture or the ethos of their academic institution. The positivistic orientation is therefore not politically innocent. By looking away from the human damage produced by their society, scholars committed to objectivity produce knowledge that disguises the human suffering in their midst and legitimates the status quo of their society. This kind of positivism, Dumont warns, can even influence the doing of theology. To be respected at the university as a scholar of the human sciences, a theologian may be tempted to engage in exegetical, historical, or systematic studies as a detached specialist. Positivism, our author argues, makes the real world of people disappear. Truth here disguises relevance.

Against positivism Dumont insists that scholars engaged in scientific research must have a critical understanding of their culture. This is true to some degree even in the natural sciences: the paradigms scientists employ in their research have a relation to their cultural context. Critical attention to their culture is even more important for social scientists and historians. Since the questions researchers ask have a profound impact upon their findings, they must be aware of where their questions come from – from the dominant culture or from their critical reflection on that culture? To gain a critical perspective of one's culture, Dumont argues, one must listen to the people recounting their experience. New insights, creativity, and social movements start at the community level. Our author holds that intellectuals who do not listen to what is happening on the ground quickly become ideologues, unconcerned about people's unresolved problems. Dumont insists that the social sciences are related to ethics – to the recognition of evil and the affirmation of the good.

Dumont's critical social science has an affinity to the preferential option for the poor adopted by liberation theology – the commitment to read society from the perspective of the poor and give public witness in support of their struggle for justice. According to the Frankfurt School, unless the scholars make "an emancipator commitment," their theories and conclusions will simply confirm society as it is, despite its injustices and its violence. This intrinsic connection between knowledge and ethics recalls the sentence of Saint Augustine: *Nemo intrat in veritatem, nisi per caritatem.*[6] In a famous interview, Max Horkheimer, the founder of the Frankfurt School, argued passionately that by being blind to ethics, positivistic science offers no guidance to society.[7] "From the scientific point of view, hatred, despite its different social function, is not worse than love. There are no scientific grounds why I should not hate, if by doing so I do not damage my position in society." While he himself was not a believer, he had hope and respected the promises of religion. In this interview he said, "Everything related to ethics is ultimately grounded in theology, not in secular reasoning, even if theology is derided today." For him, just as for Dumont, the inkling of Transcendence is the source of humanization.

The theology of interpretation is of practical importance to the believing community. According to Dumont, as we have seen, the biblical figures continue to address the anguished questions of this community and provide inspiration for creative responses to them. Working out these responses is the task of the theology of interpretation taken on by simple believers (first degree theology) or by professional theologians (second degree theology). We saw that Tradition with a capital T was for Dumont the rereading of the history of faith and the recovery of memories that address the urgent ethical and existential questions of the day. Meeting Jesus on the way to Emmaus (Lk 24:13–35), our author argues, was for the disciples a mediating event that re-interpreted for them the history of salvation, made it relevant to their present situation, and communicated to them hope and power.

Dumont's distinction between the three interacting ways of doing theology instituted a framework for the exercise of theology in the traditional sense: the exploration of the cognitive content of divine revelation. Here "faith seeking understanding" refers to the intellectual effort to uncover the intelligibility of Christian faith. Our author always feared that systematic theology would encourage the idea that divine revelation was a set of truths to be accepted and that the quest for the intelligibility of the faith would disguise the relevance of the redemptive message. By introducing the three interrelated ways of theology, Dumont created a context in which careful attention is given to the cognitive content of divine revelation without obscuring the living relevance of God's Word. In this context, the pursuit of systematic theology is honoured because it is seen as serving proclamation and open to the re-interpretation of Scripture and Tradition.

Systematic theology explores the cognitive content of divine revelation in dialogue with secular thought. In antiquity theologians listened to various forms of Platonism, and from the thirteenth century on they drew upon the philosophy of Aristotle. The decision of Leo XIII to make the neo-Thomism produced in the nineteenth century the Church's official theology and philosophy prevented theologians from engaging in a sympathetic dialogue with modern thought. John Paul II's great gift to the Church was his encyclical *Fides et Ratio* of 1998, which abolished the philosophical monopoly of neo-Thomism and encouraged the exploration of theology in dialogue with modern thinkers. Despite this declaration of philosophical pluralism, the ecclesiastical authorities often still make use of neo-Thomism as if it were the Church's official theology and suspect of infidelity theologians who, disagreeing with neo-Thomism, hold that divine revelation transcends concepts defined as dogma by the Church.

Dumont's philosophy of communication, developed in dialogue with phenomenology, deals in an innovative way with the expression and the handing on of religious experience, a communication that transcends conceptualization. Because Dumont is sometimes accused of overlooking the importance of doctrine, his recognition of conceptual truth and his defense of systematic theology in chapter 6 deserve special attention. This independent philosopher is a man of faith, and as such, embraces, freely and without compromise, the Catholic tradition.

Concluding Remarks

This book is not a synthesis of Fernand Dumont's theology. It is a summary and interpretation of his *L'institution de la théologie* that tries to bring out its practical meaning and its relevance for contemporary society. Dumont has written two other books on theology,[1] he has published many articles on theological topics,[2] and he has explored the meaning and power of religion in his anthropological studies of culture and society. It is regrettable that no symposium has ever been held to bring together theologians interested in exploring the various aspects of Dumont's theology. Nor does there exist a collective volume that deals with the many-sidedness of Dumont's theological thought. Two useful articles on his theology were written by René-Michel Roberge[3] and Anne Fortin.[4] Julien Massicotte's *Culture et herméneutique*,[5] while not concerned with theology, renders a great service to theologians who try to understand Dumont's high-flown philosophical discourse. After his untimely death in 1997, the major books of our author were republished as his *Œuvres complètes* in five volumes. I am convinced that Dumont's entire work remains an important source of reflection for contemporary intellectuals in general and Quebec thinkers in particular. I say this, even though my own theological orientation differs somewhat from his.

In this concluding chapter I wish to comment on three aspects of Dumont's theology that have impressed me and deserve careful attention. I also wish to add few critical remarks.

THREE BRILLIANT INSIGHTS

I

There is first of all his conviction that no clear dividing line exists between secular culture and religious faith. To gain an understanding of society, Dumont's social philosophy draws upon categories such as faith, memory, love, hope, and transcendence, categories that he also uses to render an account of religion. The meaning of these categories in the two contexts may not be identical, yet their significance is very similar. Because secular people have a faith, draw upon a tradition, cultivate expectations, and reach out for goals that are unrealizable, they are close cousins to religious people who share these attitudes and purposes, albeit on a different level. The affinity between the secular and the religious reveals itself for Dumont also in the human quest for knowledge. For him, there is no radical discontinuity between reason and faith, nor between science and theology. Faith is prior to all forms of knowledge. The sciences rely on beliefs they have received from the culture in which they are situated, unless they have been oriented toward a new horizon by an innovative faith. Because of the priority of faith in scientific investigations, theology based on religious faith is not an anomaly at the university, but has a structural resemblance to the sciences.

Dumont's phenomenology of the sciences opposes philosophical positivism and the non-reflective positivistic mood that permeates many university departments. Because his thought challenges the monopoly of techno-scientific reason – characteristic of the present, even in Quebec – Dumont's influence on the social sciences has been limited. Some of his colleagues, puzzled by his turn to theology, have attributed this concern to his penchant for poetry and myth-making. These secular critics overlook the scientific rigour of Dumont's religious thought and his demonstration of the structural similarity between science and theology.

2

Of great significance is Dumont's idea that the faith of the believers is the source of the Church's vitality. While the leadership of popes, bishops, and priests is important and the mediation of theologians indispensable, they do not create the life of faith. Believing is a gift of the Spirit to individuals who, thanks to this gift, discover themselves as belonging to a community and as rooted in a tradition. Faith is highly personal, yet not individualistic. Faith is eager to celebrate the Good News in the community of believers, willing to be guided by the Church's ordained teachers, and, when in doubt, ready to renew itself through reflection on the Scriptures and attention to the history of the witnesses.

Dumont is aware of the pastoral significance of this insight. He repeatedly mentions that in the past, people became believers because faith was mediated to them by the culture to which they belonged. Yet in modern society, cultures of wall-to-wall religion no longer exist. Our author agrees with the American sociologist Peter Berger, who predicted that the religious pluralism of modern society would have an impact on the faith of Christians. Being surrounded by alternative beliefs, they would embrace their own faith as their personal choice and show respect for the religious convictions of others. Charles Taylor, in *A Secular Age*, also insists that in modern society to believe in God is a personal option, the free embrace of a divine gift, a matter of personal conscience. The pastoral consequences of this cultural development are considerable. In a lecture on the Church of tomorrow, I offered this brief description.[6]

Since the institutions and symbols of society are secular, people will have to decide for themselves if they want to be believers and follow a religion. They will follow their own conscience. Even if they regard faith as a gift, they must make a decision to receive it. Making up their own minds, they have to trust their own judgment. Trusting their own judgment does not mean that religious believers are individualists who are unwilling to learn from others. They may actually long for a spiritual home in which they can share their convictions and find support for their faith. Yet because trusting their own judgment is important to them, they look for a spiritual home where they are free to express their convictions and have their words taken seriously. If they choose to follow a religious organization, they will continue to obey their own consciences, speak their minds, and object to the required unanimity. Today, believers emphasize the aspects of religion that help them and stimulate them spiritually, and disregard aspects that do not correspond to their spiritual aspirations. The Canadian sociologist Reginald Bibby refers to this phenomenon as "religion à la carte."[7] This may not be a good image. For people pick out what they want to eat following their tastes, while people's choices in religion are guided by their spiritual aspirations, which can be an anguishing process.

In his reflections on the role of the magisterium, Dumont recognizes that in today's pluralistic society, Catholics follow their own consciences formed in the believing community, even if this means dissenting from the official teaching. Armand Veilleux, the Quebec Cistercian currently Abbot of Scourmont Abbey in Belgium, fully agrees with Dumont's analysis. Today, he writes, Catholics have respect for ecclesiastical authority and are willing to learn, yet since they trust their own judgment, they also want to speak and be heard. The Vatican offers its teaching, Veilleux continues, as if the

believers still lived in Catholic cultures, embraced the entire
doctrinal system, and avoided dialogue with outsiders. He
writes, "The Church tries to be present to a world that no
longer exists."[8] With Dumont, Veilleux recognizes that in
modern society a certain pluralism within the Church has become inevitable. The sociological studies of Martin Meunier
and his colleagues have documented this diversity in the
Church of Quebec.[9] In this new setting, the pastoral task of
the ecclesiastical government is to define and promote the
Church's unity in Christ and in his Spirit. This task is shared
by the entire believing community.

3

The pastoral effort to protect and foster the Church's unity is
greatly helped by Dumont's reflection on the various ways of
belonging to a collectivity. He has shown that believers are
and remain Catholic by symbolic identification (*la référence*)
with the redemptive events recorded in Scripture, the religious
experience of the early Church, and the witnesses of faith
throughout the ages. This includes the liturgy, the practice of
baptism, and the Eucharist, as well as the public confession of
the Creed and the Gloria. Dumont calls these saving messages, rites, and acts the Church's Tradition with a capital T.
This symbolic identification is strengthened by the witnesses
to truth and compassion offered by contemporary Catholics,
in particular by their leaders, the bishops and popes. Pope
John XXIII confirmed *la référence* by the respect and sympathy he had for ordinary men and women, following Jesus'
example, and by seeing himself as one of them, despite his
high office. His defense of people's dignity and freedoms
made Catholics discover a new dimension of the Gospel and
re-identify themselves with the Catholic tradition.

The secular analogy for membership in the Church, Dumont
has argued, is belonging to a nation or a country. We identify
ourselves with the origin of our country, the great events in its

history, the struggles in difficult times, and its great leaders, thinkers, and artists. Even if we disagree with the government, we remain committed to our country, confident that it has resources for becoming more just and more humane than it is at present. In a similar way, though on a different level, we are Catholic by memory and hope. We remain identified with the events of salvation and the cloud of witnesses throughout history, even if we do not agree with certain pastoral policies of the ecclesiastical government. Today vast numbers of Catholics remain unconvinced by the papal teaching on women and human sexuality; they find the Anglican teaching more persuasive. They also regret that the Church's hierarchy has stepped back from its commitment to social justice made in the 1960s and 1970s. Yet these disappointments do not diminish the symbolic identification of Catholics with the Tradition with a capital T. Being Catholic continues to be for them the source of new life, mediating communion with God and solidarity with the human family.

As I mentioned in a previous chapter, Dumont has great respect for Protestant Christianity. His ecclesiological reflections apply also to the Protestant tradition. Believing Protestants belong to their Church by *référence*, by symbolic identification with the redemptive history which includes the liberating events of the Reformation. I believe that Dumont's analysis of belonging actually applies to all religious traditions. The memory of the great spiritual events throughout their history becomes for believers the foundation of hope and the source of strength.

CRITICAL QUESTIONS

I

In his *L'institution de la théologie* Dumont does not deal with the effect the secularization of society will have on the exercise of academic theology. For him the location of theology is the university. Theologians are to be in dialogue with secular thinkers and become engaged intellectuals. Yet he does not seem to ask himself what the future of academic theology will be in a society that is becoming increasingly secular. Fewer young people will want to study theology: vocations to the priesthood have rapidly declined, and since the educational system in Quebec has been secularized, Catholic theology is not longer taught in the public schools. Employment for theologians is becoming scarce. Nor are we assured that secular society will continue to spend public funds on university faculties of theology. The institutional shrinking that is taking place threatens the survival of academic theology.

It is significant that Dumont has great respect for the theological reflections of believing men and women and draws attention to the wrestling with theological issues in poetry, novels, and plays. He refers to this as first degree theology, distinct from the second theology produced at the university.

2

Problematic also is Dumont's omission of an interpretation of the conservative movement (encouraged by the papacy) in the Catholic Church. It is easy to document the measures taken by the popes to undermine the collegiality of the bishops and the relative autonomy of the regional Churches: they include removing the jurisdiction of episcopal conferences, controlling the liturgy and the pastoral policies of the regional Churches, limiting the participation of the laity in liturgy and church government, and promoting the cult of personality of the Roman pontiff.[10] There has been a return to a monarchical understanding of the papacy.[11] But this is not all. The ecclesiastical effort of restoration is freely embraced by a considerable sector of the believing community. Sectarian religion, currently spreading in all religious traditions, sees itself as the single pillar of truth, is impatient with internal dissent, looks down upon other religions, avoids dialogue with outsiders, and refuses partnership with human reason. How are we to interpret this movement?

Dumont regards the faith of ordinary believers as the source of the Church's vitality. His experience during the Quiet Revolution and, especially, his work as president of the Dumont Commission have convinced him that Quebec Catholics have a faith that is open to the world, respects the plurality of religions, and encourages cooperation with non-Catholics in building a more just and more humane society. Dumont has taken for granted that in the present age, ordinary Catholics reject the authoritarian religion they have inherited and enjoy their own relative autonomy in today's Church. He pays next to no attention to the conservative current in today's Church.

Our author's thesis that the faith of the believing community is the source of the Church's vitality and creativity may have to be qualified. Max Weber made a useful distinction between priestly and prophetic religion, the former oriented towards stabilizing the community, and the latter judging the injustices of the present and creating hope for a better future. Prophetic movements remain minorities. I suggest therefore that the Church's power to respond creatively to historical obstacles is derived from the faith experience of a minority within it. In Dumont's terms, *le dédoublement* takes place among a small number. This prophetic faith experience may initiate a renewal movement in the Church that at times is able to transform the institution. But to produce stability in the Church, the ecclesiastical government will soon foster priestly religion, emphasizing good order and obedience. Dumont hints at this when he acknowledges that the Church, like all big institutions, produces an ideology to legitimize its existence and create stability, sometimes even disguising the meaning of the Gospel. With Johann Baptist Metz, Dumont wants the entire Church to become prophetic, critiquing the societies of the world by its own faith-based and hence more humane institutional life.

3

An attentive reading of chapter 5 of *L'institution de la théolo-*
gie has convinced me that Fernand Dumont can be read in
different ways, as a conservative thinker attached to the memory of the past and as a socialist reformer who finds in the
past support for his ethics of solidarity. The ever-changing
power relations and social conditions may make it impossible
for a thoughtful critic to be fully consistent over the years. In
chapter 5, our author adopts a conservative critique of modern society, following Ferdinand Tönnies and Max Weber,
insisting that the ever-increasing bureaucratization of society
undermines the traditional institutions and the loyalty they
have produced, such as the family, the parish, the school, and
even the political party and the labour union. In chapter 5
Dumont presents the present crisis of society as *une décul-*
turation, a loss of values, destabilizing the institutions that
produce humane order in society. He even suggests that the
emphasis on human rights and freedoms transforms contemporary society into a giant shopping centre, where people buy
the goods that promise to make them happy. A conservative
nationalist could cite a few paragraphs of chapter 5 to declare
Fernand Dumont a political ally, calling upon Quebecers to
put new life into the institutions of the past.

The Dumont of chapter 5 is not the Dumont of chapter 4.
Nor is the conservative reading in agreement with the books
and articles in which our author offers a critique of modern
society that names the unjust distribution of wealth and
power and laments the humiliation inflicted upon people
pushed to the margin. With the review *Maintenant* in the
1960s, Dumont called himself a socialist. In his book *La vigile*
du Québec of 1971, he discussed at length the kind of socialism that was appropriate for Quebec, in keeping with its
ethical and political inheritance. In his *Raisons communes*
of 1995 he denounces the growing inequalities and patterns
of exclusion in Quebec society,[12] and in *Une foi partagée* of

1996 he declares that on account of these injustices Christians are unable to be reconciled to society as it is.[13] Only a careful study of Dumont's social and political thought will be able to uncover how our author brought together the Marxist and Weberian critiques of society.

We saw that in chapter 4 Dumont looks upon tradition, not as the past remembered by the dominant culture, but as the past seen by the rereading of history in the light of the moral exigencies of the present. The memory that is important for him are the words and events of the past that sustain people of the present who are wrestling to overcome the alienating impact of the conditions imposed on them. Tradition provides memory and hope. Quebecers want to remember how their ancestors struggled to retain the religion, the culture, and the language they had inherited; how men and women in religious orders fostered solidarity and cooperation in society; how the Patriots fought for the creation of representative government; and how subsequent leaders continued to nourish the ideal of political self-responsibility. In chapter 4, rootedness in tradition is not a conservative ideal; rootedness is rather a source of creativity and hope. The dreams and struggles of their ancestors support people in their present effort to remake their world. As the ancients experienced transcendence in their personal and social realizations, so – Dumont holds – does the nation experience a pull to realize itself in the present.

What conservatives and socialists have in common is that both produce a critique of liberal society and its values. Conservatives do this by comparing present society to an idealized image of the past, and socialists do it by comparing it to an idealized image of the future. Among the basic ideas of Dumont mentioned in my first chapter is the concept of the imagination taken from Gaston Bachelard. Here the imaginative capacity of the mind is deemed greater than the power of human reason. The great achievements of human reason have been anticipated by the imagination expressed in dreams, ideals, yearnings, and illusions. Our author recognizes the role played by utopias in the making of human history. In his *La vigile du Québec* he presents his own commitment to socialism as utopian. He writes, "Today's societies have never been as much in need of a utopia."[14]

Notes

CHAPTER ONE

1 Fernand Dumont (with Yves Martin), *L'analyse des structures so-
ciales régionales: Études sociologiques de la région de Saint-Jérôme*
(Quebec: PUL, 1963).

2 Fernand Dumont, *Le lieu de l'homme* [1968] (Montreal: Fides,
1994); *La dialectique de l'objet économique* (Paris: Éditions
Anthropos, 1970).

3 Fernand Dumont, *Chantier: Essai sur la pratique des sciences de
l'homme* (Montreal: Hurtubise HMH, 1973); *L'anthropologie en
absence de l'homme* (Paris: Presses universitaires de France, 1981).

4 Fernand Dumont, *Génèse de la société québécoise* (Montreal:
Boréal, 1993).

5 Fernand Dumont, *Raisons communes* (Montreal: Boréal, 1995).

6 Fernand Dumont, *Pour la conversion de la pensée chrétienne*
(Montreal: Hurtubise, 1964); *L'institution de la théologie* [1987],
in Œuvres Complètes, tome IV (Quebec: PUL, 2008); *Une foi partagée* (Montreal: Bellarmin, 1996).

7 Fernand Harvey et al., eds., *Biographie générale de Fernand
Dumont: Œuvres, études et réception* (Quebec: Les presses de
l'Université Laval, 2007).

8 Martin Roy, *Une réforme dans la fidélité: La revue Maintenant
[1962–1974]* (Quebec: PUL, 2012).

9   Gregory Baum, "The Dumont Report," in *The Church in Quebec* (Ottawa: Novalis, 1991), 49–64.
10 Maude Bonenfant et al., eds., *Le printemps québécois* (Montreal: Écosociété, 2013).
11 Dumont, *L'institution de la théologie*, 336.
12 Charles Taylor, *Modern Social Imaginaries* (Durham, NC: Duke University Press, 2002), 183.
13 "Qu'est-ce que la culture, si non le sens conféré à l'univers par des personnes humaines afin qu'elles s'y rassemblent, qu'elles définissent des normes d'action et de savoir, qu'elles y interprètent leur histoire?" Dumont, *L'institution de la théologie*, 309.
14 Gregory Baum, "Science and Commitment: Historical Truth According to Ernst Troeltsch," in *The Social Imperative* (New York: Paulist Press, 1979), 231–54.
15 Dumont, *L'institution de la théologie*, 348–9.
16 Fernand Dumont, *La vigile du Québec* (Montreal: Hurtubise, 1971), 138.
17 Dumont, *Le lieu de l'homme*, 181.
18 Julien Massicotte, *Culture et herméneutique: L'interprétation dans l'œuvre de Fernand Dumont* (Quebec: Nota Bene, 2006), 112.

CHAPTER TWO

1   Dumont Commission, *L'Église du Québec: Un héritage, un projet* (Montreal: Fides, 1971).
2   Gregory Baum, *Truth and Relevance* (Montreal: McGill-Queen's University Press, 2014), 28–32.
3   Vatican Council II, pastoral constitution *Gaudium et Spes* (1965), #44.
4   John Paul II, encyclical *Sollicitudo Rei Socialis* (1987), #15.
5   É.-Martin Meunier, *Le pari personnaliste: Modernité et catholicisme au XXe siècle* (Montreal: Fides, 2007).
6   Dumont, *Une foi partagée*, 178–81.
7   *Gaudium et Spes*, #5.
8   Janice Newson, *The Roman Catholic Clerical Exodus* (Toronto: Toronto University Press, 1976).

9 Max Horkheimer, *Die Sehnsucht nach dem ganz Anderen* [The Longing for the Totally Other] (Hamburg, Germany: Furche, 1970).

10 Cited in Maurice Zundel, *Dans le silence de Dieu* (Quebec: Anne Sigier, 2002), 160.

11 Émile Durkheim, *The Elementary Forms of Religious Life* (New York: Free Press, 1965), 474.

12 Gregory Baum, *Man Becoming* (New York: Herder & Herder, 1970/Seabury Press, 1979).

13 Benedict XVI, encyclical *Caritas in Veritate* (2009), #78.

14 Farid Esack, *Qur'an, Liberation and Pluralism* (Oxford, UK: Oxford University Press, 1997).

15 http://www.vatican.va/roman_curia/congregations/cfaith/documents/rc_con_cfaith_doc_20000806_dominus-iesus_en.html (accessed 27 September 2014).

16 Gregory Baum, "L'Église catholique et le dialogue interreligieux: un Magistère incertain," in *Le dialogue interreligieux*, edited by Fabrice Blée and Achiel Peelman (Montreal: Novalis, 2013), 201–18.

17 http://www.vatican.va/holy_father/benedict_xvi/speeches/2011/november/documents/hf_ben-xvi_spe_20111119_corpo-diplom_en.html (accessed 27 September 2014).

18 Jean Bédard, *Maître Eckhart* (Quebec: Stock, 1998); *Nicolas de Cues* (Montreal: Hexagon, 2001); *Marguerite Porète* (Montreal: VLB éditeur, 2012).

19 Bernard Émond, *Il y a trop d'images* (Montreal: Lux, 2011).

20 Mark Lewis Taylor, *The Theological and the Political* (Minneapolis: Fortress Press, 2011).

21 Roy, *Une réforme dans la fidélité*.

22 Fernand Dumont, *Récit d'une émigration* (Montreal: Boréal, 1997).

23 Baum, *Truth and Relevance*, 153–5.

CHAPTER THREE

1 Dumont, *L'institution de la théologie*, 233.

2 Leo XIII's encyclical *Aeterni Patris* of 1879 made the thought of Thomas Aquinas the Church's official theology and philosophy.

3 Paul VI, Constitution on Divine Revelation *Dei Verbum* (1965), #2.

4 The decree on Ecumenism *Unitatis Reintegratio* (1964), #11.

5 Dumont, *L'institution de la théologie*, 241.

6 Bédard, *Maître Eckhart*, 181.

7 Baum, *Truth and Relevance*, 53–4.

8 Dumont, *L'institution de la théologie*, 184–90, 225–6.

9 Pius XII, encyclical *Humani Generis* (1950), #21.

10 Vatican Council I, Constitution *Dei Filius* (1870); see Henricus Denzinger, ed., *Enchiridion Symbolorum* (Freiburg i.B, Germany: Herder, 1963), #3013.

11 Synod of Bishops (1971), "Justice in the World," in David O'Brian and Thomas Shannon, eds., *Catholic Social Thought* (Maryknoll, NY: Orbis Books, 1992), 288–300, esp. 295.

12 US Bishops (1986), "Economic Justice for all," #358, in *Catholic Social Thought*, 572–680, esp. 662.

13 "S'il en est ainsi, on ne définira pas le magistère comme l'unique titulaire des normes de la foi, ni même de sa régulation. Il n'a jamais été, et n'est pas non plus aujourd'hui, un simple producteur de documents. Le pape, les évêques sont d'abord, par leur activité pastorale, des gardiens d'un héritage et d'une unité qui débordent des textes." Dumont, *L'institution de la théologie*, 222.

14 Franz König, *Open to God, Open to the World* (London: Burns & Oates, 2005), 138–9.

CHAPTER FOUR

1 Dumont, *L'institution de la théologie*, 263.

2 "Lorsqu'on ne s'y abandonne pas, quand on accepte de se fier au souvenir et à l'espérance, le projet consent à la durée tout en tentant de lui conférer un sens. Pour y arriver, le projet doit se référer à une transcendance. La conscience de la finitude le suppose par elle-même: je ne l'éprouve que si je confronte ma condition à quelque représentation d'un infini." Dumont, *L'institution de la théologie*, 268.

3 The Parent Commission, instituted by the Quebec government in 1963, produced a five-volume report that reflected the values of the

Quiet Revolution. It recommended that education be recognized as a right for all young people, that it be financed by the government, and that new schools and universities be built. See Claude Corbo, *L'éducation pour tous: Une anthologie du Rapport Parent* (Montreal: Presses de l'Université de Montréal, 2002).

4 Dumont, *Une foi partagée*, chapters 7 and 8.

5 "La mémoire du chrétien n'est pas promise à la quiète possession de la certitude. Elle est, et l'étymologie le suggère parfaitement, *fidélité*. Elle est habitée par le doute, son indispensable fécondité. Cette mémoire ressemble à toutes les autres fidélités: elle est vivante de par ses incertitudes mêmes, et c'est pourquoi elle demeure attentive non pas seulement à Dieu, mais à la finitude, comme au double signe de son authenticité." Dumont, *L'institution de la théologie*, 269.

6 See John XXIII, encyclical *Pacem in Terris* (1963), #5 and #10 respectively.

7 Charles Taylor, *A Secular Age* (Cambridge, MA: Harvard University Press, 2007), 126–7.

8 This quotation from the 18th volume of Herder's *Werke* is cited in F.M. Barnard, *Herder's Social and Political Thought* (Oxford, UK: Clarendon Press, 1965), 100.

9 "Pour ce qui est de la conscience religieuse, les gens de mon âge ont vécu au Québec une mutation semblable. Nous avions reçu la foi par des traditions familiales et des pratiques culturelles quasi unanimes; en grandissant, nous pressentions l'univers d'une Église plus vaste que celle de la maison ou de la paroisse, mais selon une continuité sans failles. Vint la crise religieuse: la désaffection d'un grand nombre, les contestations: alors, il a fallu dépasser les traditions, sans les renier, mais pour accéder à une conscience historique de la foi." Dumont, *L'institution de la théologie*, 273.

10 Ibid., 274.

11 *Dei Verbum*, #12.

12 *The Catholic Catechism*, art. 110.

13 Benedict XVI, *Jesus of Nazareth: From the Baptism in the Jordan to the Transfiguration* (New York: Doubleday, 2007); *The Infancy Narratives* (New York: Doubleday, 2012).

CHAPTER FIVE

1 Gregory Baum, "L'Évangile, source de l'engagement social," in Gregory Baum, ed., *Pacem in Terris – Paix sur la terre* (Montreal: Novalis, 2013), 19–24.

2 *Gaudium et Spes*, #62.

3 This phrase is an adaptation of the second sentence in Jean-Philippe Warren's *L'art vivant* (Montreal: Boréal, 2011).

4 See pages 51–2.

5 Max Weber, *The Protestant Ethic and the Spirit of Capitalism* (New York: Charles Scribner's Sons, 1958), 181.

6 Alexis de Tocqueville, *Democracy in America* (New York: Random House, 1945), 366.

7 Dumont, *La vigile du Québec*, 103–62.

8 Ibid., 154.

9 Dumont, *Raisons communes*, 171–86.

10 "Significative est la multiplication des cultures parallèles. Aux Églises s'opposent, dans leur sein ou à l'extérieur, les sectes et les petites communautés. Aux vastes systèmes médicaux font contre-partie les groupes dits d'autosanté. En marge des réseaux officiels de la littérature, de l'art, de l'information se créent des lieux de production plus restreints. Cette défection des appartenances fa-vorise la croissance et l'expansion de nouvelles formes de pouvoir. Dans la mesure où les organisations politiques, religieuses, scienti-fiques gonflent leurs mécanismes et leurs effectifs, les pouvoirs s'en dégagent plus nettement. Le fossé s'élargit entre la culture des initiés et la culture des communautés des hommes." Fernand Dumont, *Le sort de la culture* (Montreal: Hexagone, 1995), 34–5.

11 Dumont, *Raisons communes*, 199–207.

12 Ibid., 204.

13 Étienne Plamondon Émond, "Le Québec est une référence," *Le Devoir* (31 March /1 April 2012).

14 "Pendant que l'État-providence retenait surtout l'attention, mainte-nant que les hommes politiques exaltent sur toutes les tribunes l'importance de l'économie et donc de la société marchande, la col-lectivité québécoise se reconstruit par le bas après avoir été secouée

dans ses fondements. Alors que les utopies du Grand Soir ont fait long feu, cette utopie-là, beaucoup plus discrètement, gagne constamment du terrain." Dumont, *Raisons communes*, 205.

15 Lise Baroni and Yvonne Bergeron, *L'utopie de la solidarité au Québec* (Montreal: Paulines, 2011).

16 Dumont, *L'institution de la théologie*, 325.

17 Johann Baptist Metz's first book introducing his new political theology is *Zur Theologie der Welt* (Mainz, Germany: Matthias-Grünewald-Verlag, 1968), in English translation, *Theology of the World* (New York: Herder & Herder, 1969).

18 Baum, *Truth and Relevance*, 77.

19 Dumont, *Une foi partagée*, 178–81.

20 Cited in Dumont, *L'institution de la théologie*, 330.

21 "Pour que s'instaure un espace public où la liberté des uns n'opprime pas celle des autres, où se reconnaisse la promotion des personnes par rapport à un bien commun dont tous puissent se réclamer sans se l'approprier, la nation, l'État, le droit apportent leur contribution respective. Mais chacune de ces composantes d'une société vivante est à la fois ouverture sur la transcendance et fermeture sur soi. Toutes les institutions publiques sont ainsi à double versant. D'une part, ce sont des donnés, des organismes avec leurs déterminations propres … D'un autre côté, les institutions publiques représentent la communauté inachevée, toujours en chantier, lieu et moyen de la concertation. Rien n'est assuré d'avance dans ce double jeu." Dumont, *Raisons communes*, 214.

22 Dumont's reflections on agnostics are similar to those offered many years later by Pope Benedict XVI in his address at the meeting for peace at Assisi on 27 October 2011.

23 Gregory Baum, *Truth Beyond Relativism: Karl Mannheim's Sociology of Knowledge* (Milwaukee, WI: Marquette University Press, 1977); and "Science and Commitment: Historical Truth According to Ernst Troeltsch," in Baum, *The Social Imperative* (New York: Paulist Press, 1979), 231–54.

24 On the openness of cultures to one another, see Gregory Baum, *Signs of the Times* (Ottawa: Novalis, 2007), 57.

25 Steven Lukes, *Moral Relativism* (New York: Picador, 2008), 104.

26 F.M. Barnard, *Herder's Social and Political Thought* (Oxford, UK: Clarendon, 1965), 101, 107.

27 *World Religion, World Peace: Proceedings of the Second World Conference on Religion and Peace*, Louvain, Belgium, 28 August–3 September 1974.

28 Benedict XVI, Homily on 19 April 2005. http://romancatholicblog. typepad.com/roman_catholic_blog/2005/04/thanks_to_willi.html (accessed 27 September 2014).

29 Assemblée des évêques catholiques du Québec, "Est-ce que toutes les religions se valent?" 16 June 2005.

30 Gregory Baum, "Benedict's Jerusalem Message on Religious Pluralism," *The Ecumenist* 46 (Summer 2009): 1–4; "Interreligious Dialogue: A Roman Catholic Perspective," *Global Media Journal* (*Canadian Edition*) 2011, Volume 4, Issue 1, 5–20.

CHAPTER SIX

1 Dumont, *L'institution de la théologie*, 356.

2 Baum, *Truth and Relevance*, 147.

3 "Toutes les figures forment le chassé-croisé d'un sens, d'une économie de salut, qui soutient les lectures des prophètes et que l'écrivain, le théologien de la Bible, rassemble et assume. Jésus est au confluent de ces figures, dont il est l'Interprète et la Réalisation." Dumont, *L'institution de la théologie*, 376.

4 "Le Christ n'est pas un concept, mais un être singulier auquel on voue sa foi dans un acte de charité qui n'épuise aucune notion; néanmoins, ce serait s'abandonner au fidéisme le plus aveugle que de ne point s'interroger sur l'identité de Jésus. Dès les origines de l'Église, les grands débats christologiques ont dû assumer cette interrogation et y répondre par le secours des concepts et des argumentations." Dumont, *L'institution de la théologie*, 383.

5 See pages 94–7.

6 "No one enters into truth, save by charity." St Augustine, *Contra Faustum*, Migne Patrologia Latina, t. VIII, xxxii/18.

7 http://www.dober.de/religionskritik/horkheimer.html (accessed 27 September 2014).

CONCLUDING REMARKS

1 Dumont, *Pour la conversion de la pensée chrétienne*; *Une foi partagée.*

2 A listing of Dumont's articles on theology can be found in the list of all of his articles in Fernand Harvey et al., eds., *Bibliographie générale de Fernand Dumont* (Quebec: PUL, 2007), 15–26.

3 René-Michel Roberge, "Un théologien à découvrir: Fernand Dumont," *Laval Théologique et Philosophique* 55.1 (February 1999): 31–47.

4 Anne Fortin, "Théologie et sociologie dans l'œuvre de Fernand Dumont: lecture de la crise religieuse des temps présents," *Recherches sociographiques*, I II, 3 (Sept.–Dec. 2011): 833–48.

5 Massicotte, *Culture et herméneutique.*

6 Gregory Baum, "The Church's Tomorrow," *The Ecumenist* 47.3 (Summer 2010): 6–10, esp. 7.

7 Reginald Bibby, *Fragmented Gods* (Toronto: Stoddart, 1987); *Restless Churches* (Ottawa: Novalis, 2004).

8 Armand Veilleux, "Qu'arrive-t-il à l'Église?" 10 Feb. 2010, http://www.scourmont.be/Armand/arm-eng-6.htm.

9 É.-Martin Meunier et al., "Permanence et recomposition de la 'religion culturelle': Aperçu socio-historique du catholicisme québécois (1970–2006)," in Robert Mager and Serge Cantin, eds., *Modernité et religion au Québec* (Quebec: PUL, 2010), 79–128.

10 Gregory Baum, "The Forgotten Promises of Vatican II," *Historical Studies* 77 (2011): 7–22.

11 Since this book was written prior to the March 13, 2013, election of Pope Francis, it does not mention that the conservative leadership of Benedict XVI and, before him, of John Paul II in the second half of his reign has been replaced by Francis's pastoral policy to renew the life of the Church following the recommendation of the Second Vatican Council.

12 Dumont, *Raison communes*, 176–7.

13 Dumont, *Une foi partagée*, 158.

14 Dumont, *La vigile du Québec*, 138.

Index